Youth Ministry:
WHAT'S GONE WRONG
and how to get it right

"For years David Olshine has been a significant mentor and leader in youth ministry. He has not only taught about youth ministry but also modeled and lived youth ministry, and shared his insights, experience, and love for kids and families over the years. This book brings together the best of what David has taught and led for years and invites us to consider and apply what he has discovered along the way."

—Chap Clark, Professor of Youth, Family, and Culture, Fuller Theological Seminary, and author of *Hurt 2.0: Inside the World of Today's Teenagers*

"When it comes to youth ministry, I pay attention when David Olshine speaks or writes. I have known David since he was a college student. Today, thirty years later, David Olshine is one of the foremost authorities on youth and family ministry. Whether you are a youth worker (paid or volunteer), parent of a teen, or senior pastor, *Youth Ministry: What's Gone Wrong and How to Get it Right* is a must read."

—Michael Slaughter, Lead Pastor of Ginghamsburg Church and author of *Christmas Is Not Your Birthday*

"Very few people have the insight to write a book probing whether or not we are doing the right things. Dr. David Olshine has done just that as he provides a biblical and practical perspective on thirteen critical issues that need rethinking in the strategic field of youth ministry."

—Dr. Bill Jones, President, Columbia International University, Columbia, SC

"David Olshine hits it out of the park with his book *Youth Ministry: What's Gone Wrong and How to Get It Right*. In my travels, I have come to find that the principles in this book would prove invaluable for anyone associated with youth ministry. David Olshine shows how to fix the prevailing issues that we face today. What a great read!"

—Adrian Despres, Vice-President of Kingdom Building Ministries and chaplain of University of South Carolina Football

"David's passion for youth ministry runs deep. His years of experience have given him keen insight into the current issues facing youth ministry and the church. In this book he provides answers that can change the trajectory of your youth ministry. Buy this book and give it to all of your youth workers!"

—Mark W. Rowland, Senior Pastor, Anderson Hills United Methodist Church, Cincinnati, OH

"It's easy to take potshots at youth ministry and blame it for just about everything that's gone wrong with the church in recent years. I've lobbed a few of those grenades myself. But that's not what this new book is about. David Olshine accurately and briefly identifies problems that plague youth ministry today, but he spends the bulk of this book doing the hard thing—offering hopeful and biblical solutions for more effective youth ministry in the future. This is not only a great read but an encouraging and practical guidebook for anyone working with kids in the church today."

—Wayne Rice, Pastor to Generations, College Avenue Baptist Church, San Diego, CA, and co-founder of Youth Specialties

Youth Ministry:
WHAT'S GONE WRONG
and how to get it right

d a v i d   o l s h i n e

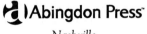
Abingdon Press™
Nashville

YOUTH MINISTRY: WHAT'S GONE WRONG
AND HOW TO GET IT RIGHT

Copyright © 2013 by Abingdon Press

Library of Congress Cataloging-in-Publication Data has been requested.

ISBN 978-1-4267-5773-0

All names and significant details have been changed by the author to protect the identity of individuals.

13 14 15 16 17 18 19 20 21 22—10 9 8 7 6 5 4 3 2 1
MANUFACTURED IN THE UNITED STATES OF AMERICA

CONTENTS

FOREWORD

Dave Olshine and I go back a long way. I certainly wouldn't describe myself as his mentor. Our relationship is probably more Butch and Sundance than Luke and Yoda. We started out in youth ministry when youth ministry was still coming of age. Unlike the current day when it feels like there are more youth ministry "experts" than there are people actually *doing* youth ministry, none of us were experts then. We were all learning together, all making the same mistakes, and all trying to figure out if this was something we could do beyond our early twenties.

Thirty-five-plus years later, it feels like there's still a lot to learn, and we keep discovering new mistakes to make. But it's beginning to look like we just might be able to extend this youth ministry adventure for the long haul.

One of the great joys of long-term youth work is the shared journey of co-ministry, the great privilege shared by sports teammates, combat veterans, and members of the Rolling Stones (not so much the ministry part) and the privilege of standing together shoulder to shoulder in a common cause and living to tell the tales. That's what I share with David Olshine.

Dave's youth ministry experience is vast. He has seen all the fads come and go. He's been on the beach long enough to see the tides rise and fall several times. He clocked in at half-past overhead projection, took a lunch break sometime around "outreach is dead," stayed at his desk on through "Are you emergent?" and now, just as the big hand points to "the importance of family ministry," he's still working away. That, I think, is why this book is so valuable.

Folk in youth ministry can be what I call *neophiliacs*. We tend to be infatuated with the new. In some ways, that's good: it keeps us open to new ideas and methodologies, a trait that comes in handy when you're working with adolescents.

But, in some ways, it's really bad. It leads us to develop that kind of arrogance so typical of adolescents, that they're the first people to experience anything: their elders don't know anything about life, their teachers can't tell them much they need to know, their coaches don't understand *today's* game, and their parents have never had sex. It's an unfortunate mind-set that causes us to dismiss the Grand Tradition of the Church, the great books that weren't written in the last three months, and the important discoveries of missionaries, pastors, and servants of God who've walked the road before us (and the Rolling Stones!).

And all of that causes another problem: people who feel underappreciated (the youth ministry vets) tend to get cranky. So, they either get mad and take their youth ministry toys and go away to a senior pastor position, or they stick around and wring their hands about how "things have changed since the good old days when kids could appreciate the genius of 'electric chairs' and egg-in-the-armpit relays."

Rare is the veteran youth worker who can overlook being underappreciated and can recognize that his or her greatest contribution may not be in working with teenagers but in training and mentoring the next generation of people who will work with teenagers.

David Olshine is *that* kind of youth worker. Which is why I think you're going to find this book really valuable.

Dave has been around. He knows youth ministry from the front and back and from the inside out. But, he's not just some aging sage, some barnacle stuck on the pier of youth ministry. Dave is still in the game. You'll see that in these pages. He's not just a thinker (although he is certainly that); he's a practitioner. His calm, matter-of-fact approach to everyday ministry issues demonstrates years of experience in the field. And as he navigates the straits, narrows, and grand banks of ministry, we benefit from the way all of that in-the-trench experience offers ballast for the voyage.

But, he also has a mentor's heart. He's not some grumpy old guy complaining about how "all these young folk with their Apple products remind me of Eve in the garden!" David Olshine is a teacher, a teacher who deeply believes in the potential of his students, a teacher who understands that, though there may be arrogance and some goofy questions along the way, the great responsibility of those who have learned is to pass along their wisdom to those who don't yet know. These pages witness to his many years of training youth workers and youth ministry undergraduates at Columbia International University. We see it in his simple, practical explanations, his gracious, good-humored realism, and in his sound, field-tested know-how. One at a time, in plain language, he addresses everyday youth ministry problems with this simple format—step one: let's talk about what's wrong; step two: let's talk about how to fix it.

Before you begin to explore these issues, let me just say one more word about your guide. Dave Olshine is not just a man of experience and a man willing to share that experience; he's a man of passion. This isn't just his book; it's his mission. As a husband, a dad, a professor, a mentor, a youth worker, and a friend, Dave has fleshed out what it means to be faithful to Christ. And I'm excited that people like you and me can read a book like this and be exposed to people like him.

We'll all keep learning together, and we'll probably keep making mistakes. But, I'm confident this book will help cultivate cool heads, steady hands, and strong hearts so that the next generation of youth workers is prepared for a lifetime of fruitful ministry.

On the adventure of grace,

Duffy Robbins
Professor of Youth Ministry
Eastern University
St. Davids, Pennsylvania

ACKNOWLEDGMENTS

Youth Ministry: What's Gone Wrong and How to Get It Right is thirty years in the making. It started simmering in my twenties, percolating in my thirties, and boiling over in my forties. Now that I have entered my fifth decade, I am so grateful to those who have shaped me into the person that I am still becoming.

I know that by the time this book comes out, I will realize that I have forgotten or left out some names, so forgive me. Please know that if we have rubbed shoulders, there's a great chance you have affected me.

To those who mentored and inspired me in the areas of leadership: Dr. Joseph Bishman, Mark Rowland, Michael Slaughter, Dan Hawk, Blair Lerner, Daniel Miller, and Steve Moore. Professors Dr. Robert Coleman, Dr. Donald Boyd, Dr. Ken Kinghorn, and Dr. Don Joy. Thanks for imprinting the gospel on my life.

To the men and women who have forced me to think deeply about youth ministry issues: Rick Bundschuh, David Burke, Jim Burns, Chap Clark, Mark DeVries, Doug Fields, Craig Garrison, Stuart Hall, Ray Johnston, Jeff Kersey, Chris Little, Helen Musick, Tic Long, Ginny Olson, Kara Powell, Wayne Rice, Duffy Robbins, Ginny Olson, Rich Van Pelt, Keith Wasserman, and the late Mike Yaconelli.

A special section of each chapter is referred to as "Voices from the Trenches." Trench Writers, thanks so much for your insights: Wes Andrews, Jeff Baxter, Carsten Bryant, Terrace Crawford, Andy Cunningham, Andrew Hedges, Karen Grant, Chris Ledley, Kristina Killman, Trevor Miller, Brent Metcalf, Barry Russell, Ainslee Stanford, Jason Lamb, Madison Reke, Sam Rubinson, Keith Seymour, and Grace Marie Ward.

To the young leaders I have had a chance to work with in ministry: Nick Cunningham, Daniel Hobbs, Andy Charles, Todd Milby, Jonathan Weibel, Matt Densky, Jamie Smith, Edward "Rudy" Farmer, Wes Carnley, Tyler Baker, Jacob Tedder, David Clifton, and Dustin McGriff. The future of ministry is bright because of you.

Acknowledgments

Special thanks to my youth ministry professor team at Columbia International University: Karen Grant, Sam Rubinson, and Brandy Stevens.

To Richard and Melba Jackson for the use of your beautiful getaway home near Charleston where I could write in peace. Thanks for your generosity!

To my soul brothers, Larry Wagner and Julian (Father Hule) Goddard who love and challenge me continually, and their voices speak even when they are not present.

To my mom who allowed me to be a kid growing up and to my sister, Emily, for bailing me out of college before I ditched the whole thing.

To Chic and June Weisman for being the best in-laws ever!

To my incredible wife and best friend, Rhonda, for more than three decades of blissful marriage. You are the best! Thanks for the encouragement.

To my children, Rachel and Andrew. You bring me great joy. I love you!

Finally, to Yeshua my Messiah, who makes me alive and gives me joy and purpose each day.

Chapter One

WHATEVER HAPPENED TO PARENTS?

> *"I don't have the knowledge or time to help my teen*
> *with spiritual things."*
> —mother of a fourteen-year-old

I have a confession. I love youth ministry.

Yet inside my soul is a love-hate relationship with what's happening in the church today. Let me explain, because I am troubled.

I love the universal church, and I have spent most of my adult years doing youth ministry. When you love someone, or something, it enables you to be affirming and critical in order to make changes and improvements. Take marriage for example. I have been with my wife, Rhonda, in a wonderful adventure for three decades, and in order to maximize our relationship, weekly we look to see the good things we have going for us. Then on occasion (okay, on multiple occasions) we analyze and critique the way we listen, communicate, and share life together. We do this because we love each other and don't want our marriage to grow drab, ineffective, or out of touch. We seek to discover new ways to keep the fires burning and the commitment, intimacy, and friendship alive and growing. Evaluation is essential to making sure things are on the right track.

The Bible compares the church (body of Christ) and marriage (Ephesians 5). In the same way Rhonda and I took vows before a congregation of more than six hundred friends and family (and others who wanted free food) "to love and to cherish in sickness and in health." Part of loving and cherishing each other in marriage is not being afraid to identify the weaknesses of the relationship and to come up with solutions. The same approach is taken in this book as it pertains to youth ministry.

The reason I am writing this book is that I deeply care about teenagers, paid youth workers, parents, and volunteers, and I want us to get better at what God has called all of us to do. In fact, I have given my heart and soul to youth ministry!

There is much that is *right* about youth ministry. We have some great leaders in the youth ministry world along with some fantastic resources and innovative and creative organizations. We offer super conferences and seminars and host some amazing events and outreaches. And when it comes down to intentionally hanging out with students and building personal relationships, few do it better than youth workers! Anytime individuals and groups surface who love teenagers and want to see them grow in a relationship with Jesus, it's a good thing!

What's the Problem?

Let me first stop and affirm that a number of youth workers—paid and nonpaid servants—highly appreciate and value the parents of their teens. But from my perspective, one of the most troubling issues in American youth ministry is our current approach of not partnering and empowering the parents of youth. I believe this silent but enormous elephant in the room can no longer be ignored. We have to address this topic before we head down the road of no return.

Problem #1 of American Youth Ministry
Excluding Christian parents from their God-given purpose and calling.

How Have We Excluded Parents?

We often exclude parents because of our own insecurities. My friend Paul Borthwick calls it "parent-noia," a deep-seated fear and anxiety of parents. We in youth ministry have sometimes made parents adversaries rather than allies. Why? We can be intimidated by parents, and some parents are a little scary! And yet parents are not the enemy; they are on the same team with us, trying to influence teens for great impact.

We exclude parents because of the tradition of "payroll entitlement." It is easy for a church to say, "We will *hire* a person to care for our students. We will pay you to shepherd our sheep (teenagers) and provide you with two weeks' vacation, a pension, continuing education, and a medical package. Your job is simple: evangelize and disciple teens and have a solid support system with good adult volunteers. Take care of our kids!" Initially that sounds fabulous, but two things are missing in that job description. First, there is no mention of parents, and, second, the job seems ultimately dependent on the paid youth worker to "get the job done."

Most of us were trained to work with students only. The title of youth director or youth pastor pretty much states the obvious: we are working with students, and that is our mission field. And if the sense of calling is primarily to teens, oftentimes youth workers think that partnering with parents is something for another person to take on and guide.

The past few decades have seen an escalation of activity in the youth program. I believe teens need their time and space with one another, but when we start establishing two or three weekly youth group meetings, plus retreats, camps, and conferences, perhaps it sends a message, "Parents, please stay away." The youth program has become an island unto itself and a sacred cow.

Finding a Solution

Based on the authority of God's written Word, the Scriptures, we see that God-fearing parents are the cornerstone of depositing faith in their children. I believe youth ministry has oftentimes unknowingly contributed to the breakdown of parents' role in the discipleship of their children.

In the book of Deuteronomy, we are introduced to what is known as the *Shema*. At the heart of the Judeo-Christian faith, the clarion call is to "love the LORD your God with all your heart and with all your soul and with all your strength" (6:5). Moses spoke these words from God, and Jesus affirmed this text also to communicate one foundational truth: *God-fearing parents are to be the primary nurturers of their children's faith.*

Even today, the Shema is prayed three times a day in Orthodox Jewish homes and is central to the formation of a child's purpose in life.

Do We Believe Parents Are Primary?

One youth worker whom I interviewed, named William, told me this:

Our youth ministry started believing that parents didn't think about spiritual nurture for their children, so we took on the baton of leadership.

3

It was a huge mistake. My team started taking on the role of "spiritual parenting." Parents will naturally abdicate their spiritual role if the church wants to run with it. In the long run, this is what started to burn me out.

William is not alone.

We have some decisions to make as youth workers. Will we believe the Bible's instructions for families to lead their children to know God deeply, or will we move the baton away from parents?

God's book is clear: spiritual training is primarily and directly driven and motivated first and foremost by faith-driven parents to their kids—not by the church or synagogue, not by the clergy or paid youth workers. Listen to the words of Moses that are often missed in Deuteronomy 6:6-9:

> These commandments that I give you today are to be upon your hearts. Impress them on your children. Talk about them when you sit at home and when you walk along the road, when you lie down and when you get up. Tie them as symbols on your hands and bind them on your foreheads. Write them on the doorframes of your houses and on your gates.

The words that jump out from the text for me are these: "Impress them on your children"; "Talk about them"; "At home"; "When you walk"; "When you lie down"; and "When you get up."

Spiritual formation is primarily transferred from parent to child; it is from generation to generation.

Solution to Empower:

We need to find ways to give the ball back to Christian parents—where it belongs—as the primary spiritual caregivers of their teens.

Where Does Nurture Take Place?

After I became a dad, I took this challenge seriously. I have two children who are amazing, but that does not mean parenting is simple; it's not. But man, has it been rewarding!

As a father I desperately wanted to be a "Deuteronomy six dad"—to spiritually care for my children. Early on it dawned on me, "I need help from the body of Christ, from mentors and others who would also help shape my kids. I cannot do this alone." I am grateful for the youth pastors and spouses and our school and friends and family who supplemented my role.

I needed the additional help from others. Yet, I see no mention of the collective gathering of believers doing the *primary* job of disciple-making (although the Scriptures stress the importance of "other influencers" to young people, which will be addressed in future chapters). It was my job and that of my wife, Rhonda, to be the head chefs in the kitchen.

Parents are commanded to have God's Word on their "hearts" first and then are to "impress" Scripture on "your children." I love the natural flow of how this happens, of talking about God at home—when you are walking to a baseball game, going to bed, and eating Cheerios for breakfast.

The main place of spiritual nurture and connection is the family—parents dispensing, forming, loving, and shaping their kids. The bone I am picking is this: American youth ministry has not done an effective job in *assisting* parents to prepare their children to love and know God. One of the famous lines from the Apollo 13 mission was, "Houston, we have a problem." Well, American youth ministry has a big problem.

Voices from the Trenches

"In my middle school years, my parents encouraged me to study and memorize passages like 1 Corinthians 13 and Philippians 2. Our curriculum was based around the faith. History included ancient heroes of the faith and people like Blaise Pascal and the great hymn writers, D. L. Moody, and Billy Graham. Equally important, this was a time when my curiosity in science began to lead me to conclusions drawn by scientists that were far different from the lessons I had learned in Sunday school. It wasn't the church we attended, youth pastors, or small-group leaders who led me to the books like *Mere Christianity* or *The Case for Christ*. It was my parents who bought the books and were willing to talk to me about them. They nurtured me to be able to have a faith for myself."

—Carsten, High School Student

Reality or Excuses?

So why do I have a love-hate relationship with the church I love? Why do I stress over American youth ministry, which I have sweated blood and tears over for almost thirty years?

My love-hate relationship is related to expectations. For years, I have heard all the reasons and excuses about why parents cannot lead their kids spiritually: "Parents are apathetic about their kids' relationship with Jesus"; "Parents are too busy"; "Parents don't even crack open their Bible, so why should their kids?"; and "My dad probably thinks John 3:16 is a bathroom on the third floor."

Maybe you are not convinced that youth ministry is contributing to this problem of parental removal in teens' spiritual development. Consider these questions:

- Would you agree that many parents are not spiritually nurturing their kids?

- Would you confirm that a number of parents are too busy to even try?

- Or that the single parent is worn out?

- What about the "average Christian parent" who is extremely intimidated with the thought of reading the Bible together as a family, much less explain it?

- How about the parent who tries to create a "devotional time" with great intentions but the children push back and look bored?

I think I am hearing a yes to all the questions I have just raised, so what on earth do we do to mend this problem?

Biblically Motivated?

I believe the Bible is true, and I know that it's practical. I have seen parents step up to the plate and lead their students. I know most Christian parents can nurture their kids if given the proper tools and motivation. I have witnessed the power of God when parents lead their kids to grow in their friendship with God. I have watched hundreds of parents who didn't know what to do ask for help, and changes were made. I have seen youth ministries partner with parents to make a difference. Yes, parents can be empowered to be the spiritual leaders of their teenager.

Can youth ministry help resolve this problem? Will we find ways to give the ball back to parents? I answer with a resounding *yes!* What does it mean to be an empowered parent? Here are ten practical strategies to push us to get it right:

1. The church needs to affirm and vocalize that Christian parents are the most important spiritual influencers for their children.

The problem was exacerbated when preachers and leaders started saying, "The church is the primary place to be for children and youth." You might respond, "I've never heard someone say that." Maybe not, but many church leaders guide their congregations as if *life* depended on spending hours being involved in the local church building. The way some ministries function on a daily basis would lead us to believe that the church is the main instrument of change in the lives of children and youth.

I have heard well-meaning pastors during baptism ask the congregation to recite promises and vows to support the child being immersed, sprinkled, or drenched with holy water, followed by the question, "Who is responsible to see that this kid grows up to love Jesus?" The leader says out loud, "We are." But I don't find the Scriptures proclaiming that the church is the primary instrument to help a kid grow to maturity in Jesus.

I have heard key leaders in the American church say, "The local church is the hope of the world." That sounds nice and good, but where is that in the word of God? The church needs to say it loud and clear: "The mission of God in reaching children is primarily through parents, not through youth group or the church." Don't get me wrong, I believe children's ministry is vital and youth ministry is important, but they are *supplemental* in walking with Christian families.

The analogy could be stretched further to include the role of schools, government, sports, medicine, and extracurricular events in the lives of teens. I am grateful that our children have other people "at the table" to impact and add other voices of wisdom to their minds and hearts, but when it comes down to ultimate influence, that is the role of a parent. The guidance of the other voices is secondary, not primary.

A renewed mission for American youth ministry needs to be clear: *to empower parents to be the primary spiritual nurturer and caregiver of their kids.*

Voices from the Trenches

"Parents are the greatest influencers on their kids. Parents by their very position and role are building values, ideologies, and beliefs in their children. The relationship between parents and children has no equal."

—Chris, local church paid youth worker and parent

---

2. Let's acknowledge that teens do want a relationship with their parents.

I have been guilty as a youth pastor in trying to run a program that pushed parents away, sometimes not even knowing it. I wonder how many youth workers have made youth group an American idol.

As a paid youth pastor, I have attended many sporting events to support students in my youth ministry. I have always enjoyed knowing that one of "my kids" on the court or gridiron has spotted me in the crowd. Yet deep down in the soul of a young person are the eyes that scan the audience. Who do they really want to see in the stands? They are looking for Mom and Dad.

Most teens do respect their parents and want a relationship with their mom and dad. As a pastor, professor, youth and family counselor, I have lost count of the number of times I've heard these aches and cries from teens, college kids, and adults: "My dad never came to one of my basketball games"; "Why was Mom's job more important than me?"; "They just don't care about anyone but themselves"; and "I can't believe Dad missed my graduation." Young people desperately desire a relationship with their parents, and youth ministry needs to do all it can to make sure that happens and not go against the grain.

Voices from the Trenches

"The Scriptures call parents to be the primary spiritual nurturers of their children. It's something that was engrained in the mind-set of Israel and reinforced as the church grew (Acts 2:39; Ephesians 6:4). The larger spiritual family is absolutely essential to reinforce the training in the home but is never called to replace it. In consideration of a young person coming from a home without believing parents, the larger spiritual family 'adopts' these into nurturing relationships (1 Timothy 1:2; Titus 2) with the prayerful goal of seeing the whole household loved into the family of faith."

—Andrew, paid youth worker and parent

3. Youth ministry must not compete for family time.

How many times have you seen youth workers plan events over spring break or summer, which, unbeknownst to the youth leader, is running major competition with the family? The teen must choose between youth group and the parent, which is not an easy choice to make. If the young person chooses the church event, then the parents sometimes feel like they are losing the battle. If the student chooses to vacation with the family, some youth workers will throw a guilt trip on the teen for "not being committed to Jesus."

My youth pastor friend Jack said, "I would be a much better youth pastor these days because I've been on the other side of the fence as a parent now and understand their plight more than I did when I was a young youth pastor with no kids."

Voices from the Trenches

"Parents are contagious. Habits, sayings, and ways of life tend to transfer to their children because they're building on it 24/7. Loving Jesus is often a contagious thing as well. Putting the two together can cause major life change! If parents have a passion for God, their children are likely to be following in their footsteps by catching the fever. Once the ball starts rolling, children start asking their parents spiritual questions they might not ask any other time other than when it pops into their head. This begins to form a relationship that is so much deeper than just a love between a parent and child. Suddenly, a common love of a Savior is shared."

—Madison, high school student

---

4. Youth ministry programs must complement the good values parents are teaching at home.

Have you ever heard a youth worker contradict a parent? I have. It is unsettling and arrogant. Youth ministry must uphold the values of the family, even if we disagree with the manner or the methodology. Some paid youth workers have no children of their own, so they really have no idea of the magnitude of what it means to be a parent. Instead of trying to understand the values of a family, some youth leaders will criticize the parents in front of the teenager.

This can lead to a disaster waiting to happen. So if you recognize the vital necessity of seeing youth and their parents connecting, then at least develop *programs* while keeping parents in mind. Programs that can benefit parents as well as youth should be considered; avoid programs that might alienate parents. Consider offering specific mother-daughter and father-son events, movie nights, or baseball games for families. Provide retreats, seminars, and potluck meals and prayer nights for families. Listen to parents' hurts and needs and program accordingly. Consider nonthreatening events and, yes, even some nonspiritual programs for parents who are not interested in church or Christianity. Two of my favorite events are: (1) parent-teen messy game night and (2) broomball, in which you rent out an ice skating rink, put on your tennis shoes, and play with brooms and an old volleyball. Also remember that events such as roller-skating and ice-skating are just fun ways of watching people fall down! When you program, try and coincide with families' calendars rather than conflict with them.

5. Parents want a youth ministry that is family friendly and sensitive to their finances.

One of the insidious problems we must be aware of is being non–family friendly. What does that look like? An overabundance of programs, late nights, and all-night lock-ins (the invention of some crazy youth worker) can be a huge barrier to teens and their parents connecting better. When teens are constantly at the church building, attending youth group or Sunday school while their parents are elsewhere, this is not the way God intended it to be. When the pace is out of control and parents are running their kids from event to event, this is not family friendly.

Additionally, expensive, over-the-top events, retreats, mission trips, and concerts can become a financial burden on families and their priorities. If the youth ministry is planning events, from time to time consider something that is free and not time-consuming. Whatever happened to simply playing Frisbee in the park or swimming in the lake?

6. Parents want a youth ministry that will walk with their kid but not replace their role.

Not too long ago I had breakfast with a parent of two teens and asked him, "What do you want out of a youth ministry?" He responded, "I want them to support us but not try to be the parent. That is *our* job." Many parents do want church youth workers to be present in their kids' lives—especially in times of crisis—but youth workers are only seasonably in the big picture of an adolescent's full-fledged life. Youth ministry needs to find ways to cheer on parents. Being a parent can be a thankless job. How about having a Parent Appreciation Night? Youth ministry is called to walk with students and families but not replace them.

Voices from the Trenches

"One Sunday I was asked to speak on the importance of God's view on shaping and molding families, I explained that Scripture holds parents responsible for teaching the Bible and passing on a spiritual heritage to their children (Deuteronomy 11:18-19; Psalm 78:1-7). The church (including youth workers) should support families. When I was leaving the facilities, I had a single mother of a teenager tell me after the service, 'That was the first time I ever heard it was my responsibility to teach God's word to our kids, and I have been in church my whole life.'"

—Karen, professor of youth ministry, family, and culture

7. Youth ministry must provide resources, counseling, and healing to parents of teens.

Parents don't always recognize what to do when it comes to raising their children with Christian values and a biblical worldview. Even with the incredible amount of information available from the Internet, most parents of teens don't know where to turn for practical help. An effective youth ministry will place relevant materials and resources into the hands of not just teens but also their parents. Here are a few ideas for educating and resourcing families.

- Provide parent newsletters with timely tips on youth culture and parenting.

- Throughout the year invite parents to attend youth group or an activity to observe what is happening in the youth ministry.

- Create a book club with the latest and best magazines, books, DVDs, blogs, and websites on parenting teenagers.

- E-mail devotional Bible readings and applicable links or texts.

- Have ongoing recommended book lists on understanding and connecting with teens.

- Host a seminar for parents of teens (see information on "Understanding Your Teenager" seminar at Homeword.com).

- Offer a once-a-year parent-teen retreat (Friday night and Saturday or all day Saturday).

- Provide support groups for parents.

- Recommend small groups for parents on topics relevant to their life stages.

- Twice a year host informational meetings for parents, giving them a yearly calendar of youth ministry activities, information on upcoming youth trips, and their costs.

- Utilize prayer chains/e-mail lists for parents.

- Occasionally take parents out for meals with the youth staff.

- Enlist a parental advisory board (parents who have a keen investment in the youth program).

- Encourage teens and parents to worship together as a family.

- Bring in speakers who can communicate practically with parents.

Voices from the Trenches

"It comes down to sheer numbers. The amount of time a parental system has with a student far outweighs the amount of time spent with any form of church influence. Parents are primary teachers to their children because if parents don't do it, the chances of their kids' spiritual formation taking root dramatically decreases. The second reason why parents are primary is because God has set that up as the way in which children should be introduced to the God who is faithful to all generations. Proverbs 3:11-12 says that the relationship of the parent to the child actually mirrors the relationship God desires with the child. Unlike any other persons in a child's life, parents have the opportunity to introduce them to their Creator."

—Trevor, paid youth worker and parent

8. Youth ministry cannot afford to ignore family systems.

We can help provide stability where there is stress and pain in the home. Some of youth ministry's greatest moments come in crisis—such as when a teen is in critical condition and we are present at the hospital, or a student commits suicide and we preach at the funeral. Parents in fact do want us to be around in tough times, for not only does it give us credibility, but also it reveals that youth ministry does matter.

Most men and women go into youth ministry to focus primarily on youth, but once a person spends any amount of time working with students, it becomes painfully obvious that there are tremendous needs and hurts within the family systems that cannot be ignored. We are called not just to minister to teens but to helping families (we will discuss this more in chapter 11, "Family Matters: More Than a Youth Worker").

9. Healthy youth ministries always point teens and families to following Jesus.

One time a teen (Michael) shared a hurt with me and asked, "What would you do if you were me?"

As I probed a bit further, my question was, "Do your parents know what you are dealing with?"

He responded, "No, they couldn't handle it."

I said, "What if you and I go talk with them together?"

That afternoon there was incredible reconciliation and healing. It was probably the first time Michael prayed with his family about something significant and pressing. Everything points back to the home and the values that derive from the family system. Great youth ministries help parents live out the gospel with their kids in authenticity and can aid families in growing their kids spiritually. Healthy youth ministries look for ways to encourage homes that have limited or uninformed access when it comes to knowing God and following Jesus.

10. Acknowledge the exception to the rule scenario called "The Middle."

Currently in American youth ministry are two extreme positions when it comes to parental involvement—Full-Tilt Youth Worker and the Family-Driven Faith Model. What's in the middle responds to the extremes of contemporary youth ministry. Look at the continuum below:

The Middle

Full-Tilt Youth Worker　　　　　　　**Family-Driven Faith**

The *Full-Tilt Youth Worker* is the classic youth leader who feels that God wants him or her to focus primarily on students, although every now and then he or she throws in a few events to help parents and families. The extreme concentration is primarily *students focused.*

The *Family-Driven Faith* is on the opposite side, and it propagates that there should be no more age segregation, no church nurseries, no kids or youth programs, no paid children or youth workers. They should all be worshiping together and saying, "Why can't we just love one another?" The extreme concentration is primarily *family focused.*

Both extremes have pros and cons, yet a healthy and biblically balanced youth ministry will have trouble camping out at one of those extreme positions. It is challenging, but the most productive ministries will seek to walk in the balance of biblical tension, primarily guided by one principle called *the exception to the rule.*

The Ten Commandments were given to the people of Israel and set up a belief and behavioral standard that differentiated them from the Ammonites, Jebusites, Amorites, Perizzites, plus Mosquito-bites, Tick-bites, Budlights (still with me?). The command to pass the faith down to the people of God in Deuteronomy 6 and Ephesians 6 is also to the followers of Jesus. The Bible is a book for people of faith, and so we cannot expect non-Christ followers to spiritually nurture their kids. They can love their children and provide for them, but they will probably not likely have devotionals for breakfast! That is why there is a *middle group* that youth ministry must be aware of and work with the tension of the extremes. The middle looks a little like these case studies:

- Christian mom and Christian dad with non-Christian kids

- Christian kids with both parents who have little to no faith

- Married couple, one with deep Christian faith and conviction and the other noninterested

- Divorced mom with no faith and a Christian kid at home, with an ex-spouse dad who is a person of faith

- Troubled teen with "troubled" parents

- Nonbelieving kids and nonbelieving parents

- A Christ-following teen who leads his parents to faith

As much as we in youth ministry desire for parents to run the spiritual show at home, let's ask, as my former student Chris Leiby asks, "What's wrong with the middle?" We need a biblically balanced approach to working with all the different kinds of families, or we will polarize students or parents.

Teens Who Do the Faith Solo

I began this chapter by suggesting that youth ministry has to figure out how to give the spiritual responsibility and accountability back to families. We have discussed the biblical model is for parents to raise their kids for spiritual training. Let me restate it again: *Christian parents are the primary spiritual nurturers of their families; the church and youth ministry is secondary and supplemental, not vice versa.*

But who nurtures teens who are raised *without* Christian or biblical wisdom and preparation? Who helps the teenager who comes to Jesus when her parents are not interested or supportive? What do we do with those in the *middle?* I believe this is where the pendulum shifts. I have insisted that Christian parents train and educate their kids in moral and scriptural views and values.

We cannot, however, expect a *non-Jesus-following parent* to carry the mantle of Christian leadership. At these times, the church and youth ministry must become—although not ideal, at least for a season—more than supplemental or secondary. They must actually become the major nurturer and supporter of the teenager who wants to grow in the faith when the parent does not.

Since the teen's parents are a little in the dark on spiritual matters, the young person looks to the community of faith as his or her extended family because the support is lacking at home (more on this later in chapter 10). Youth workers, volunteers, other parents, mentors, and peers become very much like surrogate parents for a short period of time. It is not ideal, but it is essential that all teens in the family of God are cared for in their spiritual growth.

Building Time

From start to finish, the Bible stresses the high value of families. For instance, "Then the family heads of Judah and Benjamin, and the priests and Levites—everyone whose heart God had moved—prepared to go up and build the house of the LORD in Jerusalem" (Ezra 1:5). Families went up to build the house of the Lord.

When I started youth ministry in a paid role, I was fresh out of seminary. I was newly married with no children, and I thought parents didn't know anything. At twenty-six years of age, my view was this: "Parents of teenagers are ignorant and clueless." I believed my calling was to minister to teenagers, and that is why my job title was "youth director." I didn't care much about parents and felt that they were a nuisance, not to mention that I was scared to death of most of them.

Then I became one of those "ignorant and clueless" parents. Now with two children of my own, I realize the *huge* importance of families and parents (especially fathers) doing what they are called by God to do.

My perspective has changed since those days from families being "zeroes" to "heroes." I know that many homes are messed up, but American youth ministry has created somewhat of a barrier, a wall between teens and their parents. As Ezra and Nehemiah were about tearing down walls and rebuilding them properly, let's go about getting it right.

The key to doing effective youth ministry has been right in front of our noses: *parents.* How in the world did we think that students could ever become fully functioning members of society without the help of their parents?

Though some families have abdicated their God-given spiritual authority to lead their children, that doesn't change the fact that parents are to be the primary nurturers of the spiritual development of their kids.

Parents have the most influence, so it makes sense to train them in what matters the most: having a real and genuine faith with Jesus Christ. Let's get it right by giving the ball back to the parents—to be the primary spiritual caregivers to their kids.

Voices from the Trenches

"A youth worker's role should be to come alongside parents and help with the process of nurturing teenagers. One of the biggest failures in youth ministry has been our lack of partnership with parents in the spiritual formation of their children. The reality we must face is that our time with teenagers is relatively short. We have an incredible opportunity to invest in the lives of teenagers, but it pales in comparison to the investment of a lifelong parent.

"Teenagers will graduate from our ministries, but they will always have their parents. If we are going to be effective in nurturing teenagers, we must foster a partnership with parents in which they take the lead in the spiritual growth of their children."

—Brent, paid youth worker and parent

Q's to Empower

1. What steps does your youth ministry need to take to empower parents to be the primary spiritual nurturers for their kids?

2. Does your youth ministry need to eliminate or reduce anything in order to meet families' needs and schedules? Explain.

3. What is one event/program your youth ministry can do this year to empower parents?

Chapter Two

WHERE HAVE ALL THE LEADERS GONE?
(FOR SHEPHERDS' EYES ONLY)

*Many shepherds will ruin my vineyard and trample down my field; they will
turn my pleasant field into a desolate wasteland. It will be made a wasteland,
parched and desolate before me; the whole land will be laid waste because
there is no one who cares.*
—Jeremiah 12:10-11

One of my most memorable childhood experiences happened when I
was ten years old. It was my first time on water skis. Four of my friends invited me out on the lake, and to be honest, I didn't want to go. I was not raised
on the lake and felt a little uncomfortable with the process, not to mention
the intimidating thought of climbing out of the boat and trying to ski.

By four in the afternoon, it was *my time* as my friends piled on the
abuse: "Be a man, Olshine, go on out," they shouted in unison. I reluctantly
jumped out of the boat and into the water. The entire series of events took
me about forty minutes: getting the skis on my feet and keeping them on,
signaling to the boat driver that I was ready to go, then finally standing up
on my skis.

Complicated.

When the boat started with some speed, I actually got up, and within
seconds the guys were pointing and yelling, "Go to your right" (and I was
thinking *shark?*). They wanted me to go over the wake, so I did. I jumped
and landed. But then I hit something (maybe a rhino, I'm not sure), and I

18

went flying. Now, the guys in the boat forgot to tell me one important rule: let go of the rope. I didn't let go.

The boat pulled this little seventy-two-pound kid about seventy-five yards before I realized I'd better release. When I dropped the rope, I recognized two things: my skis were gone and my swim trunks were gone (it's not funny). Even the fish said, "Yuck."

It was a painful climb back into the boat.

Did I mention I was ten years old?

It wasn't until I turned seventeen that I tried water skiing again. (I kept my swim trunks on because I used a staple gun to keep them on. Just kidding.)

Fear does funny things to us, doesn't it? Fear paralyzed me for seven years. No way was I ever going water skiing again.

What fears do you have when it comes to reaching the next generation? These students are the church **leaders now and in the future.**

What's the Problem?

I served almost two decades as a youth pastor, and as a lead pastor for almost seven years, so I know the difficulty and issues in each role. I also know the time and toil it takes to work out the senior pastor–youth pastor relationship. These positions of authority and power can clash when working together, but that doesn't mean they cannot work in unity and synergy.

I have worked with church staffs, finance committees, elders, deacons, deaconesses, district superintendents, and bishops. I have consulted with churches and have worked alongside leaders of Fellowship of Christian Athletes, Young Life, Youth for Christ, Campus Crusade, and Navigators. And because of these varied experiences, I have seen that leaders in the global church have the ability to make things happen unlike anyone else.

This chapter is specifically targeted *toward senior leadership*—men and women at the top of an organization, para-church ministry, or local church who have been given incredible wisdom, responsibility, and authority to make daily decisions that impact hundreds of people.

We must address the problem the body of Christ (the universal church) has in becoming *impotent in attracting and keeping young people.* I think this is related to ineffective leadership in nearly all congregations and organizations. We (including myself) have become so *inward* in our approach to ministry that we have too often leaned toward "insiders" rather than "outsiders."

In the American church, fear often rules. Senior leadership cannot let fear dominate. Things stall or are thrown into motion in direct proportion to the involvement of senior leadership. If you are a paid senior pastor, executive pastor, or head elder, are on a church board, or are a finance committee member, consider how vital your role is in reaching young people.

Jesus told us to be "fishers of people." Where do the fish hang out? In water: lakes, ponds, rivers, oceans. We need to start tracking where teens hang out in the same way fishermen look for bass or trout. Where are the fishing spots of young people? If we want to reach them, we cannot hide out in our offices anymore. We must go seek and save the lost. Find out where students spend most of their time (sporting events, parties, with friends) and be intentional about reaching out. Be incarnational! Relational ministry is the most effective way of connecting with young people.

What's leadership to do? If we go back to biblical times, God has always had leaders—some who led appropriately and others who did not. Still today there are good and bad leaders. Some are assertive, and others are reluctant; some have strong convictions, and others are misguided.

Senior Leadership Has Become Too Passive and Safe in Reaching Out to Young People

There are two mentalities when it comes to leadership and fish-catching: *come and see* or *go and love*. On the one hand, the "come and see" method is the church (insiders) waiting for people (outsiders) to "show up" at our services. We may even invite teens to attend a retreat or concert, but that is still a passive approach. We think, "I hope they come and see what we are up to." That is the "come and see" method.

On the other hand, the "go and love" model is dynamic and active—going where young people live. Going and loving involves intentionality and initiating and building relationships with students and families that the Bible calls "outsiders" (Colossians 4:1-6). They are outside the community of faith, and our challenge is to create bonds and bridges so that they become "insiders."

Every community is different when it comes to where the "fish" are swimming. The way to find out is simple: *look around and ask*. "Where do middle school and high school students go hang out?" Leaders tend to ignore the fishing rod and bait and hope the trout and bass will somehow hop into the boat (a church meeting).

Nothing is going to happen without taking the initiative and action. Don't let fear rule you. What is at stake are the hearts and souls of a generation of lost young people!

Problem #2 of American Youth Ministry:
The shepherds and leaders in the body of Christ have become too safe in reaching out to youth.

Fearful Like Jonah?

Many leaders in the church today have emulated the prophet Jonah. A friend of mine says that we do "Jonah evangelism." Jonah was called by God to go to the Ninevites, a group hated by the Israelites. The Ninevites were not a friendly people.

I can see why Jonah didn't want to go preach to them. Jonah was being sent to Nineveh, the capital of Assyria; God was calling him on a mission trip. So guess what Jonah did? He played it safe and headed in the other direction. The Bible refers to Nineveh as a "great city" and "wicked." Going to Nineveh would have been like sending a Jewish man or woman to confront Hitler in the 1940s.

Jonah jumped on a ship heading for Tarshish (Spain), about three thousand miles in the opposite direction from his destiny. Jonah must have had resources because the cruise boat was not cheap: "He went down to the port of Joppa, where he found a ship leaving for Tarshish. He bought a ticket and went on board, hoping to escape from the LORD by sailing to Tarshish" (Jonah 1:3, NLT).

Jonah ultimately was not running from the brutality of the Assyrians or the fact that he was bigoted or self-absorbed. He was running from God and evading God's call because he was uncomfortable going to a group of people who were not on his radar.

God was in charge, and the Lord got Jonah where he needed to be. God used a storm and then a large fish to get Jonah's attention. Finally Jonah obeyed the second time and preached one simple eight-word message to Nineveh: "Forty days from now Nineveh will be destroyed" (Jonah 3:4, NLT). That was the message, with no chance for repentance or change, but Jonah knew something about God's heart and character that the reader of the book of Jonah doesn't fully understand.

The prophet's real motivation for not wanting to obey God's call to reach the unreached was a different reason. It was not for his protection or safety that he did not want to go to Nineveh. Jonah was not fearful of losing his life, because if he were, he would not have insisted the sailors throw him overboard (which would have given him a good chance of drowning). Jonah was not frightened of Nineveh; he was petrified of the mercy of God.

Running on Empty

Jonah revealed why he ran in chapter 4, "Didn't I say before I left home that you would do this, LORD? That is why I ran away to Tarshish! I knew that you are a merciful and compassionate God, slow to get angry and filled with unfailing love. You are eager to turn back from destroying people" (4:2, NLT).

Jonah ran because he knew God would give compassion and forgiveness to anyone asking for it! Mercy trumps judgment. God knew the city was great and wicked, in spiritual darkness, and could not figure out their right hand from their left. God loved this group of people whom Jonah did not care for, and God not only was trying to change Nineveh but also wanted to transform Jonah and his view of people.

Jonah needed his perspective of people altered, and so do we. Jonah's vision of God was right on target, but his view of people was shortsighted. Jonah wanted the Ninevites to be destroyed, but he knew that God moves heaven and earth to change people when they repent and obey him.

God loves and wants a relationship with all people groups.

What happened to Nineveh? "They believed God." They turned from their sin following Jonah's message of impending doom. The book closes with Jonah being angry and pouting at God and Nineveh, to which God responds, "But Nineveh has more than 120,000 people living in spiritual darkness, not to mention all the animals. Shouldn't I feel sorry for such a great city?" (4:11, NLT).

What Does Jonah Have to Do with Senior Leadership in the Church Today?

American church leadership has neglected going out to "seek and save the lost"—namely, young people. We have become too insulated as a church. We have become territorial and isolated.

Like bigoted and fearful Jonah, we have fled and gone the other way.

Finding a Solution

How big a deal are youth to the global church? When was the last time you witnessed a teen reading Scripture in "big church"? Why do some churches have Youth Sunday once a year during which they showcase youth's gifts and talents and then rarely hear or see them again until next year's big event? Why are leaders reluctant to let young people lead and learn and even mess up?

Don't be afraid of fear of reaching teenagers. Don't be afraid to fish or swim, or we might become like Jonah.

Solution to Empower:
We need God-called leaders who think critically and take risks with vision and passion.

Effective youth ministry starts with a *stirring*. We see in the book of Ezra this truth: nothing happens without leadership. Ezra 1:5 refers to "everyone whose heart God had moved." We are in great need of a God-initiated stirring to reach the heart and soul of children and youth. But something is inherently wrong, isn't it?

It all begins with leadership. In the Bible, Abraham, Moses, Joshua, Josiah, Nehemiah, Isaiah, Ezekiel, and King David were leaders, as were Paul, Peter, John, and Jesus.

I have seen churches with strong leaders who have a burden and passion to see kids who reached for Jesus do astounding things. I have also seen the other side of leadership, in which not much happens except keeping a dysfunctional system running. Sometimes it looks like this:

- Make sure the bills are paid.

- Keep the church kids happy.

- Ignore unchurched students and families.

Churches that do this remain entrenched in business as usual.

What's gone wrong? Our leaders are lacking vision. We've become too passive concerning reaching youth. How can we equip leaders to think critically and take risks?

Consider the Parable about Caution

In Matthew 25, there is a parable of the kingdom of God. The word *kingdom* is not used often in our contemporary language, but in Jesus' day *kingdom* meant "the rule and reign of God." Wherever God's rule and reign were present, the King of the kingdom was at work. Jesus told a story of a man who went on an extended trip and gave each of his servants some responsibilities. One was given five bags of gold, another was given two bags, and a third servant was given one bag. Each servant was given monies based on his abilities.

Here is how the parable played out, and it has incredible implications for the future of youth ministry:

> Then he [the master] left. Right off, the first servant went to work and doubled his master's investment. The second did the same. But the man with the single thousand dug a hole and carefully buried his master's money.
>
> After a long absence, the master of those three servants came back and settled up with them. The one given five thousand dollars showed him how he had doubled his investment. His master commended him: "Good work! You did your job well. From now on be my partner."
>
> The servant with the two thousand showed how he also had doubled his master's investment. His master commended him: "Good work! You did your job well. From now on be my partner."
>
> The servant given one thousand said, "Master, I know you have high standards and hate careless ways, that you demand the best and make no allowances for error. I was afraid I might disappoint you, so I found a good hiding place and secured your money. Here it is, *safe and sound down to the last cent.*" (Matthew 25:14-25, *The Message,* emphasis mine)

The third servant with the smallest abilities of the three and with the least amount of money hid the money. He played it safe. Why? Let's read on: "The master was furious. That's a terrible way to live! It's criminal to live cautiously like that! If you knew I was after the best, why did you do less than the least?" (25:26-27, *The Message*).

Jesus then sent the strongest message of the parable to the third servant: "Take the thousand and give it to the one who *risked* the most. And get rid of this *play-it-safe* who won't go out on a limb. Throw him out into utter darkness" (25:28-30, *The Message,* emphasis mine).

The last servant had bad thinking, not because he was a bad person, but because his theology was bad. He knew the master was a risk taker, but the servant lived in fear and cautiousness. Playing it safe will do that, creating an environment of trepidation and apprehension that keeps us from taking steps of faith and courage.

Read verse 26 again: "That's a terrible way to live! It's criminal to live *cautiously* like that!" (emphasis mine).

The servant was rebuked by the master for living *cautiously.*

Wanted: Leadership That Values Children and Youth Ministry

If Christian leaders can overcome the cautious factor, then the second principle should be quite simple. We need leaders who value children and youth ministry. The good news is that most senior (lead) pastors have *influence* to make things happen in their local context. Lead pastors can support and inspire their congregation to have a vision for youth ministry, and this can trickle down to finances and budgets being aligned with the needs of youth and family ministry.

Christian Smith's study reveals that "senior pastors rank higher than youth pastors with students when it comes to spiritual influence and long-lasting impact in their lives."[1]

If you are a senior leader in the church, you are valued. Students like you and respect who you are and what you do. You are a huge reason youth ministry is happening (or not happening). The message senior pastors need to hear is this: "You have incredible influence in the lives of teenagers, and they look to you for spiritual leadership." What an encouragement. (And you thought teens disliked you.)

Do you value seeing youth reached for Christ?

The word *value* carries the idea of "important, significant, worth, and meaning." My wife and two kids are my highest value on earth. I will do anything and everything for them. I provide for them and protect them. I just love hanging out with Rhonda, Rachel, and Andrew. We have a blast together.

Another high value for me is traveling and seeing the world. I love the adventure of getting onto airplanes, climbing mountains, and visiting new cities, states, and countries. Having fun is another high value for me. I enjoy laughter and love to play and get silly.

At the age of thirty I set some life goals, and one was to visit every state in the United States. In May of 2012 my wife and I decided to combine all three of these values and goals. I had one state yet to visit: Alaska. We took action: a Disney cruise to Alaska to celebrate our wedding anniversary. We had an amazing time together. It included three values: family, travel, and fun all in one week (yes, we let our kids come!).

Senior leaders must value children's and youth ministries if they want to reach them. Recognize that the two go hand in hand. A children's ministry is what I call a "feeder" system into youth ministry. If there is a strong children's ministry in the church, it will feed into the student ministry, and subsequently if the children's ministry is struggling, then youth ministry will probably struggle. Children's and youth ministry is like a relay team.

In the 2012 London Olympics, Michael Phelps became the all-time Olympic medal winner with twenty-two medals. For the first time in his swimming career, he anchored the 4x400 medley. By the time Phelps was ready to swim his leg, he was given a substantial lead, and the Americans won the race pretty handily. Before the race, Phelps told his teammates that he needed a big lead to hold it. He did.

The same is true in children's and youth ministry: it's a relay race, and the team that is firing on all cylinders will have a strong finish.

The Apostle Paul said in 1 Corinthians 9:24-25: "You've all been to the stadium and seen the athletes race. Everyone runs; one wins. Run to win. All good athletes train hard. They do it for a gold medal that tarnishes and fades. You're after one that's gold eternally" (*The Message*).

Are we running to win the hearts, souls, and minds of children, teens, and young adults for the sake of the cross and resurrection of Jesus Christ?

The Bible says it crystal clear: run to win!

Voices from the Trenches

"The church has become a foreign place to young people. They're not going to feel comfortable to just 'come as they are.' One thing the church can do is to support, equip, and train adults from the church who already have relationships with youth in the community—teachers, coaches, employers—and find ways to relationally connect with them."

—Karen, professor of youth ministry, family, and culture

The Church Is Aging

Recently I glanced at a seminary that is starting a degree in ministry to the aging. This isn't just a focus on geriatrics. The reality is that the United States is getting older, and the church is aging. If you haven't noticed, take a glance of those who sit in the pews.

I am preaching at my church this weekend, all four services. Two of the worship services are contemporary (Saturday at 6:00 p.m. and Sunday at 9:00 a.m.), with a full-scale band, and two services (Sunday at 8:00 a.m. and 10:30 a.m.) are traditional, with a full-scale choir of white hairs and organ! Each service targets a particular crowd and audience. Take a second and guess who will attend each service.

The Saturday night service is relaxed and will draw in "baby boomers with kids," and so will the Sunday contemporary service with various seasons of life in attendance. The Sunday 8:00 a.m. crowd is typically those who are sixty years and older. The 10:30 traditional service crowd will have mostly forty-five-year-olds and upward.

The church is aging and not getting any younger, that is, unless we decide to do something about it.

Put yourself in a teenage body and mind for a moment. Abby arrives at a Sunday morning worship service, and few if any of her friends are at "big church." Abby's first impulse is to sit down and "check out," so she starts searching on her phone for places to eat following church (who said church isn't productive for some things?). The teen sees lots of gray hairs and hears hymns sung at a melancholic tempo, and the sermon is "Why Your Finances Matter to God and Should Matter to You." At this moment, Abby has left the building (emotionally).

As Abby sits, she is wondering a few things in her head:

- Where are my teenage friends?

- Why is the church so borrriing?

- Why would any of my friends ever want to step inside the doors of this old and outdated fortress?

Try an experiment as a senior leader: treat some of the teenagers to lunch and ask them one simple question. When you are done asking, take notes and make no comments. Listen to their hearts. Teens have much to say. So listen. Have no agenda or axe to grind.

Here's the question: From your point of view, what should church look like?

Listen well and then start praying about steps of implementation. Teens are not just the church of the future, they are the church now.

Pray for New Spirit-Filled Leaders

What are you doing to recruit and equip new leaders who are open to the Holy Spirit? What are some ways in which you can connect to and then commission new leaders?

You have probably heard of the 80/20 principle—20 percent of the congregation does 80 percent of the church's work. What will it take to get people in your church to move from being spectators to being participants?

Maybe you have heard this definition of professional football: twenty-two players in dire need of rest are on a football field while sixty-five thousand fans who are in dire need of exercise watch them from the stands.

What will it take to get people out of the stands and into the game? I challenge you to think out of the box (or out of the stadium, as the case may be). Do something engaging and risky. Remember the leadership parable from Matthew 25, and avoid being cautious!

Collaborative Ministries

My organization, Youth Ministry Coaches, consults and coaches youth ministries, organizations, and churches. Out of the hundreds of congregations we have worked with, I can remember only two who connected the dots of children's and youth ministry.

What happens when children's and student ministries collaborate? First of all, vision and alignment happens. Everyone gets on the same page and pace. Second is unity. Third is continuity with programming. Last is strategy: children's and youth ministry can help transition groups of students. Take at look at the issues that Anderson Hills United Methodist in Cincinnati, Ohio, needed to think about when they brought me in as a consultant.

- How do we give parents resources for elementary-age kids?

- How do we offer parents guidance during the middle school and high school years?

- What are the needs of elementary school children? Of fourth and fifth graders?

- What groups should be together?

- Do we separate sixth graders based on the school system keeping them apart?

- Should we keep middle school and high school students together? For how long? When do we separate them?

- When and how do we transition third graders?

- At what age do we encourage church membership/confirmation for teenagers?

- How do we retain the kids in children's ministry over the summer when we are transitioning them to middle school?

These are just a series of situations to consider; and if children's and youth ministries collaborate, the synergy and creativity will be unlimited.

Voices from the Trenches

"The church needs to refocus. Speaking from my experience, most people make the decision to accept salvation in those pivotal teenage years. If the church really is focused both on evangelism and discipleship, then it needs to hone in on investing in the *next generation*. Whether this means hiring new leaders who have great vision and are willing to go ALL IN for youth ministry or having a pastor who is willing to engage with the kids and who has bought into what the youth ministry is doing, unity among all facets of the church is what is necessary for the church to become relevant again in young people's lives."

—Wesley, high school student

Intentionality about Reproducing

One of my former students is a teaching pastor in a large church in the Midwest. Recently he attended his first annual conference of his denomination. I asked him what observations he had of the event, and he said, "I was one of the youngest people in the building." Nick is almost thirty. His point is that the church is getting older. And if we are going to have any sense of relevance and staying power for the future, we must go after young leaders.

The call of the church is to "go into the entire world" and to be "the salt of the earth." The salt was meant to come out of the saltshaker, not stay in it. Jesus stressed the need for the shepherd to leave the ninety-nine sheep and go after the one stray. And we are called to go beyond the four walls of the church.

We need a new generation of Spirit-filled leaders who have a vision to reach out and go fishing. Jesus said, "I will make you fishers of people."

Be Gutsy Like Joe

My first pastor was Joe Bishman, who later became a district superintendent in the United Methodist Church. His first church (a circuit of three churches) was the tiny Central Avenue United Methodist Church in Athens, Ohio. Joe was in his late twenties and was a student attending Ohio

University, married with two kids, and trying to keep his head above water while shepherding a small congregation.

Joe is a marvelous communicator and storyteller, and with his leadership, Central Avenue UMC, located on the west side of the city, began to grow exponentially. Historically, Central Avenue was a small church struggling to survive, and due to a turn of events, it almost closed the doors of its college-town building.

God used Joe as an instrument of change in that little church. Through simple yet profound preaching, excellent music, the power of prayer, and the Holy Spirit, the audience began to grow, and guess who started to fill the pews? Young people—high school and college students—packed out that little building with great energy and faith-filled worship services. Guitars, drums, and a full band in the mid-1970s rocked that United Methodist church!

I was one of hundreds of university students who attended and participated at Central Avenue in those days, and many of us answered a call to full-time service. Renewal was happening and lives were being altered.

Why?

A man of God named Joe had a passion and vision for seeing young people make a difference.

Leaders at the top have been given incredible possibilities to change the world, and that priority and excitement toward youth and families can be fulfilled.

Senior leaders can be game changers.

Voices from the Trenches

"Students should all be allowed to 'shadow' staff, intern with staff, and sit on any committee or board in the church. The fresh-minded young people will always ask questions that older people tend to forget: 'Why do we do what we do?' 'What are we trying to accomplish by doing this event?' 'Are we effectively reaching the community?' Students in leadership across generational lines keep communication open to older generations that tend to fall into programming and planning ruts and routines. Students must be empowered and incorporated into the daily decision-making processes that are involved in the life of the church."

—Andy, bi-vocational worker in the church and marketplace

Leaders as Visionaries

Nehemiah was a common man with an uncommon vision. When he heard that the walls of Jerusalem were in ruins and the city gates reduced to cinders, he responded with tears, mourning, fasting, and prayer.

He was not a prophet or priest or teacher of the law of his day. Nehemiah was a cupbearer for King Artaxerxes, sort of like the right-hand man to the king. Nehemiah was the wine taster for the king, so if the fermented grape juice was poisonous, down went Nehemiah. It's not the kind of job many people would apply for, but it was an important duty. He was the king's secret service, so to speak.

Nehemiah heard from one of his brothers, Hanani, of the ongoing brokenness of Jerusalem, and a pit formed in his stomach. He prayed, "Make me successful today so that I get what I want from the king" (Nehemiah 1:11, *The Message*).

What did Nehemiah want? If you read on, you'll see that his heart bled for the people of Jerusalem. He wanted to return to his homeland and rebuild the walls. Vision was brewing within Nehemiah.

Leaders are dreamers and visionaries.

Nehemiah had no earthly idea how he was going to get to Jerusalem, much less how the walls would be rebuilt. But he knew that he wanted to go. Vision always precedes strategy.

Vision is about *where*—that is, where are we heading?

Mission is concerned with *what*—that is, what are we trying to do?

Strategy deals with *how*—that is, how will we accomplish the mission?

Nehemiah did not know the answers to the where, what, or how questions initially. So between the months of Kislev (December) and Nisan (April) something was marinating in Nehemiah's spirit.

What was the vision? To see Jerusalem restored as a worshiping community.

What was the mission? To rebuild the walls of Jerusalem.

Nehemiah would accomplish the mission of rebuilding in fifty-two days (see Nehemiah 6).

Leadership always begins with vision. We need men and women to sit down and weep over the broken walls of teens and families.

Don't worry about *how* to reach students. Just get on your face like Nehemiah: "When I heard this, I sat down and wept. I mourned for days, fasting and praying before the God-of-heaven" (Nehemiah 1:4, *The Message*).

Ask God for his vision to reach students and families and God will give you the where, what, and how later on in the process.

Begin with vision.

Voices from the Trenches

"I think it comes down to doing what is easy and comfortable rather than doing what is best and missional. Most churches are led by adults who are not thinking about reaching children and youth. Whether it is facility, style of worship, teaching styles or budget, children's and youth's needs are typically thought about last and are very rarely given the best.

"Part of the problem concerns how churches make decisions. Is money or the fear of losing people and their finances the most influential piece of the decision-making process? Where a church spends money is the evidence of what is important. Typically money is not spent in the areas of youth and children. We need to spend human and financial resources on children and youth! The church is in denial about the importance of ministry to youth, children, and their families, and as a result, we are losing them to the culture."

—Chris, paid youth worker

Be Vulnerable, Coachable, and Accountable

The church is in desperate need of leaders who think critically and take risks with vision and passion. How does this happen? How do we find and equip leaders? Back to Nehemiah for one more thought.

Nehemiah was an ordinary man who found himself in a stressful circumstance and wanting to turn something precarious into something brand-new. Being a leader is not sitting around and waiting for something to happen. Leaders *make* things happen. And perhaps the key is one simple principle: vulnerability.

Nehemiah was open and available, and then he approached the king with sadness (something a cupbearer wasn't supposed to do). Nehemiah was wearing his emotions on his sleeve. He was vulnerable, coachable, and accountable.

We need senior pastors, executive pastors, para-church leaders, and key lay leadership of the church to learn how to be honest and real about who they are. Wouldn't it be refreshing to have a staff meeting in which people shared their hearts, struggles, and concerns instead of simply reporting upcoming activities and events?

Some lead pastors actually started out in youth ministry. Some think they still know how to pull it off in today's world. The reality is that many pastors, church boards, and senior leaders at the top don't have a clue concerning what it takes to reach the youth culture today.

I would follow a senior leader anywhere if he had the vulnerability and coachable attitude to say, "I have not done youth work in twenty-five years, but I have the heart to see kids reached in our community. Let's have honest dialogue about what is working and what isn't. I will do whatever it takes to resource and staff this ministry to win kids and families. I don't know exactly where to start, so maybe we should pray for a while and then have a lengthy discourse. When we start, let's realize we don't all have to agree on every point. In fact, it is important to hear different sides and perspectives. All on board to dive in?"

It is time to have some vulnerability and coachable and accountable leadership from the top.

Support and Encourage Youth Pastors

All youth pastors in America want their lead pastor to care about teens and families, and many lead pastors do deeply care about students. Youth workers want to trust the senior leadership and to *be trusted* by the leadership from the top. The problems I hear from both sides can be summarized in comments like these:

- "My senior pastor and I rarely talk about anything other than baseball."

- "My lead pastor does not share much of his life with us. I was hoping to be mentored by him, but that isn't going to happen."

- "Our youth worker does not seem to care about anything in the larger church world other than student ministry."

- "I wish just once my lead pastor would ask me how I am doing (without the question being about youth ministry)."

- "We don't connect in any way relationally outside of church work" (heard from both senior leadership and youth workers).

It seems that youth pastors and senior leadership oftentimes have unrealistic expectations of one another, plus other nonverbal expectations. Let me give you an example of this: in my first church experience following seminary, I assumed my lead pastor would coach and mentor me. But his perspective (which took me over a year to learn) was that I was the "expert" in youth ministry and that he expected me to come in running hard and fast.

I did not *want* mentoring in working with students, but I needed help in managing my time, guiding a church budget, finding the best adults to be workers in youth ministry, and doing my taxes. I did not want my pastor to micromanage or be overbearing, but I did want to know that he had my back if conflicts with parents or other issues arose.

Relationships take time in order to build trust, so I asked my pastor if we could meet once every two weeks and talk about anything—ministry, marriage, football, whatever. He agreed. I decided to take the high road; if I wanted my senior pastor to support and encourage me, I needed to do the same.

Our relationship started with suspicion and competition, and within three years, my pastor and I developed a deep friendship that I am so grateful to have experienced because some youth pastors and senior pastors compete and conflict to the point of agony and no ecstasy!

The *landscape of youth ministry has changed* as well over the years. At least two decades ago youth ministry was viewed as a "stepping stone" to another ministry, like being a senior pastor, church planter, professor, or another staff role. There has been a huge swing and shift in which youth ministry is considered a legitimate lifelong, long-term profession and calling. Some people in youth ministry refer to themselves as "lifers."

Senior leadership must affirm this lifelong calling and applaud and support it.

I have seen hundreds of relationships between youth pastor and senior pastor dissolve into misery, depression, and bullying, and sometimes relationships deteriorate to the point of someone leaving the ministry and each other!

Search for common ground. You are on the same team trying to reach people. The other person is not the enemy! Encourage and support each other. This is about mutual affirmation.

If you are a senior pastor, consider taking the lead on verbal encouragement. Find ways to honor. And the youth worker needs to do the same.

- When was the last time you took the youth pastor out to eat or had coffee with him or her?

- Why not go to a ballgame together or hit some golf balls?

- Does the youth pastor know some of your struggles?

- Have you ever sat down and prayed with each other about personal life stuff and not church issues?

Voices from the Trenches

"The responsibility does not fall on the 'bigger' church alone. I believe much of the responsibility falls on the next generation. The church needs to recognize the need for younger leadership. Though it is intimidating for the church to do this, they have to realize that as their leadership ages, this next generation must take up the mantle. They need to begin to identify the leaders of the next generation, train them up, and place them in areas of leadership. The next generation needs to begin to recognize the vast wealth of knowledge available to them from the current leaders within the Christian faith and then go out to change the world."

—Trevor, paid youth worker

Strategic Leadership Needed

Nehemiah started with a vision, and then he moved forward with a strategy and direction. The king asked Nehemiah, "What do you want?" (It's a great question for all senior leadership to consider.)

Nehemiah prayed and then convinced the king that he needed to journey to Judah. The king asked significant questions such as, "How long will it take?" and "How long will you be gone?"

Nehemiah had impressive answers: "I gave him a time, and the king gave his approval to send me" (2:6, *The Message*).

Nehemiah didn't stop there. "If it please the king, provide me with letters to the governors across the Euphrates that authorize my travel through to Judah; and also an order to Asaph, keeper of the king's forest, to supply me with timber for the beams of The Temple fortress, the wall of the city, and the house where I'll be living" (2:7-8, *The Message*).

Nehemiah's vision was now proceeding toward *mission and strategy*. He knew what he needed to start the building project and was specific in his requests. And it began by convincing the top dog to put these things into motion. He knew that if the king said no, the vision would die.

Today we need senior leadership in the church to catch a vision of reaching young people and then to come up with a short- and long-term plan to implement. The greatest organizations, churches, and businesses know how to craft long-range planning. We need to put that to effective use in youth ministry.

Nehemiah was smart. He did not try to pull off this massive project alone. He learned in the process to communicate his needs, and he delegated responsibilities to the right people.

Nehemiah headed to Jerusalem, and when he arrived, he inspected the broken and burned walls: "After I had been there three days....I hadn't told anyone what my God had put in my heart to do for Jerusalem" (2:11-12, *The Message*).

Leadership is *thinking through things that have not been thought of before*. And nobody had experienced this before.

God-equipped leaders are not only visionary but also strategic and directional.

In a record fifty-two days Nehemiah and his team rebuilt the walls.

Today senior leadership can help repair the broken walls of youth and families. Let's rebuild the walls of reaching youth together by thinking critically and taking risks with vision and passion!

Voices from the Trenches

"While funding the youth group sufficiently is important, even more important is the presence of these leaders in the lives of the youth. Having older men and women actively involved in the lives of the youth as small-group leaders or mentors is probably the most effective way to reach youth. An adult opening his home and pouring into the lives of youth speaks volumes about him or her and has been a powerful thing in my life."

—Carsten, high school student

Q's to Equip

1. What would it look like if your congregational (organizational) leaders took reaching young people seriously?

2. What are some strategic steps you can take to reach youth and families in your community?

3. How can your children's ministry and youth ministry collaborate together for making long-term impact for the cause of Christ?

Notes

1. Wayne Rice, *Reinventing Youth Ministry (again): From Bells and Whistles to Flesh and Blood* (Downers Grove, IL: Intervarsity Press, 2010), 149.

Chapter Three

THE ROCK STAR YOUTH PASTOR

"As soon as enough people give you enough compliments and you're wielding more power than you've ever had in your life, it's not that you become . . . arrogant . . . or become rude to people, but you get a false sense of your own importance . . . you actually think you've altered the course of history."
—Leonardo DiCaprio, quoted in The Oregonian

When I was a kid, my parents took me to the circus. I really loved the acrobatics. I was enamored by the animals and the tricks of the trapeze artists. Watching them was amazing, and I couldn't take my eyes off their antics. The circus was so intriguing to me (although the clowns were a little creepy, not to mention the tall dude on stilts).

The one venue that always piqued my interest was the one-man show. There was a man (I never saw a woman do this trick) who dazzled the crowds as he walked around, sang a song, played a guitar, and banged on the drums. which were somehow draped around his waist, while playing a harmonica attached around his head—all at the same time! He was remarkable—kind of like a Bob Dylan in the circus. As the years have gone by, I think we have somehow taken that trick into the church. Come and see the spectacle:

THE AMAZING YOUTH WORKER WHO CAN SPEAK,

ADMINISTRATE, TEACH, PROGRAM, VISIT, AND

REACH OUT TO EVERYONE ALL AT ONCE.

What's the Problem?

Thank God the Bible does not teach the "one-person show." We are the body of Christ, made up of many people with different skills, talents, and gifts. First Corinthians 12:4-11 says:

> God's various gifts are handed out everywhere; but they all originate in God's Spirit. God's various ministries are carried out everywhere; but they all originate in God's Spirit. God's various expressions of power are in action everywhere; but God himself is behind it all. Each person is given something to do that shows who God is: Everyone gets in on it, everyone benefits. All kinds of things are handed out by the Spirit, and to all kinds of people! The variety is wonderful:

wise counsel

clear understanding

simple trust

healing the sick

miraculous acts

proclamation

distinguishing between spirits

tongues

interpretation of tongues.

> All these gifts have a common origin, but are handed out one by one by the one Spirit of God. He decides who gets what and when. (*The Message*)

Notice the phrase *each person*. All Christ followers are given spiritual gifts, not just the seminary trained or the ordained: "*Each person* is given something to do that shows who God is: *Everyone* gets in on it, everyone benefits" (emphasis mine).

American youth ministry is made up of many parts—teens, parents, adult volunteers, and staff. All have gifts and need to be utilized. If we don't encourage an "all Christians are ministers" model, we will fall prey to the next big problem in youth ministry.

Problem #3 of American Youth Ministry:
The paid youth worker's temptation is to be a rock star.

You might be thinking, "Olshine sounds so negative!" Am I being pejorative? No, I am thankful for paid youth workers! I was a paid youth worker, and now for twenty-plus years I have had the joy of training college and seminary students to work in student and family ministry.

God has gifted incredible people around the globe who have a heart to see teens become a part of the community of faith. As a professor, I have the honor and responsibility of training students to reach the next generation. I love my job because I see men and women making an impact on the youth culture. One of the most difficult tasks my team of youth ministry professors faces is convincing our college-age students that they were never called to do this job *alone*. We tell them:

- "You don't have to be perfect."

- "You will fail."

- "God wants to hold you up with his wisdom and strength."

I asked some of my college students planning to go into full-time youth ministry what comes to their mind when I say "Rock Star Youth Pastor." Here's the list they gave me:

THE ROCK STAR YOUTH PASTOR

Wants to be in the limelight; seems to gain his or her identity from ministry and not always from Jesus; desires attention; often finds himself or herself doing most of the work and loves to receive praise; wants affirmation and approval; wants to build the big show; can be insecure inwardly but cocky outwardly; is distracted by "big and better"; wants to be noticed, recognized, and famous; finds himself or herself as a lone ranger and lacks accountability to others. It's all about me. I am the main attraction.

The image of the rock star youth pastor mentioned above is *not* how it begins for us, because most youth workers I know are *not* what my students mentioned above. Nobody intends to start this way. However, the *temptation* for some of these qualities is within a lot of us. It is easy and seductive to follow the superheroes of the faith and put them on a pedestal. Youth workers are not immune from this urge for celebrity status and stardom. We see it in actors, politicians, and athletes, so why not add to the list church leaders, preachers, pastors, communicators, children's directors, authors, and evangelists?

What can we in youth ministry do to protect ourselves from this luring temptation?

Finding a Solution

There are some practical tips for overcoming the temptation to be the superstar. Sports teams with superstars don't always win championships, but *teams* do win it all. I am an avid sports fan, and when I think of such superstars as Michael Jordan, LeBron James, Albert Pujols, Wayne Gretzky, Peyton Manning, and Eli Manning, I know they were all part of a team with a supporting cast and bench players who stepped up at the right moment. There is no *I* in *team.*

Solution to Enlarge:

Take them off the pedestal, or they'll come crashing down.

Let's consider some ways to take the paid youth worker off the pedestal.

Recognize the Clash of Pride and Humility

There are numerous passages in Scripture that mention that pride "comes before a fall." All of us in leadership (and nonleadership) are vulnerable to pride. It is easy to believe our own press, to think that we are incapable of sinning in certain capacities. And that is why the remedy is humility.

Humility only comes though repentance, honesty, and confession to God and to a group of people who can hold us accountable. Most leaders think they are accountable, but they are not. The way to know is by asking these two questions:

- Who knows my heart?

- Who knows what I am struggling with?

If you cannot answer these questions, you are open to deception, and Satan loves to "steal and kill and destroy" (John 10:10). Find a group that you can bare your soul with and that will help hold you accountable. This will help you be more aware of the clash of pride and humility. As 1 Peter 5:5-6 instructs us: "All of you, clothe yourselves with humility toward one another, because, 'God opposes the proud but gives grace to the humble.' Humble yourselves, therefore, under God's mighty hand, that he may lift you up in due time."

Build a Network of Older, Wise Sages

One of my favorite weekly meetings is with three young emerging leaders whom I have sought out and two youth pastors who have sought me out. There is so much wisdom that can be given and received from all involved. I learn from them, and hopefully they learn from me.

One of my guys is almost thirty years old, and he is fantastic in youth ministry, but there are things "he doesn't know that he doesn't know." I have been trying to work with him on pacing because I have hit the wall hundreds of times and know it hurts. I can coach Barry on what it means to take time off and to get away from the office and e-mails and can advise him on being fully present when he gets home and spends time with his wife and kids.

One of the reasons younger youth leaders need older wise mentors and sages is that we can help them connect the dots and answer the "why" question. For instance, "Why are you doing this program? For what purpose is your Friday night event? What are you doing with parents, and why are you doing it?"

Youth leaders need not only to be held accountable to other staff members of the organization, but also perhaps to have some folk they trust outside of their arena of ministry. We all need people who will watch our back, and that sometimes means speaking the truth in love.

Older sages not only can help on a programmatic level but also can guide younger leaders personally, spiritually, and professionally. One of my students, at the age of thirty-nine, is asking me what can he do in the future: stay in youth ministry, start a church, be a teaching pastor, or teach college. These are the issues an older guy like me can address, by listening and coaching a younger person in ministry. I don't always give advice. Sometimes I just listen and then we pray.

Every young man and woman in ministry should seriously consider finding an older mentor (like Paul's mentoring of Timothy in the Bible). It could change your life and help kick the pedestal away.

Reconsider the Talking-Head Model

Paid youth workers like to talk, and boy can we talk! Maybe too much. We have developed a "talking-head model" in the church. Look at today's model of television talk shows. I am not saying we should take our primary cues from communication theory, but we can certainly learn from the media. Most "talk" shows consist of several people in debate, dialogue, crowd participation, audience questions, and entertaining clips.

Voices from the Trenches

"I have discovered over time that the one-man show does not work, nor does the talking-head model help equip teens and volunteers to become disciples of Jesus. Talking *at* people, in my experience, is the least effective way to engage students toward wanting to read and apply the Bible."

—Jason, paid youth worker

Whether that of anchors on ESPN or CNN political pundits, the *modus operandi* is not one person talking at an audience. It is more like this:

• Three or four people engaging one another

• Point/counterpoint and debate

• Panel in heated discussion creates a response from the crowd

The only one-person talking heads on television are TV evangelists or the president of the United States! It is one person "preaching to the choir."

Youth ministry doesn't need to completely remove the model of the talking head, because students lack knowledge and need some teaching. What I am suggesting is that youth ministry needs to *reduce* the talking-head model about 40 to 60 percent of the time. Communication at its best is *dialogical*—people going back and forth. Talking at youth is fine until they turn about ten years old. After that, lectures tend to, as the adage says, "go in one ear and out the other."

I am all for instruction and content, but teenagers need to *process and debrief* what they are learning instead of hearing a message and then walking out. If the speaker were to do less talking and more facilitating, then I believe teens would get more chances to *apply* what they are learning. And when the youth worker does not have all the answers, the pedestal is less tempting.

Have a Team of Communicators

I have been a paid youth pastor and a lead pastor of a college church and an itinerant speaker who has spoken to more than a million people in my lifetime. I know that teaching and communicating the gospel is powerful and significant. I also acknowledge that it creates incredible *pressure* and potential burnout to the paid youth worker and volunteers who do it regularly or weekly.

Paid youth leaders know the heaviness of having to convey a message, sermon, or talk three times a week (Sunday morning and night and Wednesday night). Assuming a speaker never took a break or vacation and spoke three times each week for fifty-two weeks a year, that would equal 156 talks per year (that is a lot of talking). And if you figure that a youth leader is spending eight hours a week on each talk, you do the math: that is a huge amount of hours teaching a crowd. Add to that job the stress of leading staff meetings, retreats, volunteer training, contact work with students, crisis counseling, mundane tasks, lunches with parents, and administration time. Is it any wonder that most paid youth workers' tenure is less than four years?

To get the youth pastor off the pedestal (and before he or she falls off), *let others teach*. Ginghamsburg Church in Tipp City, Ohio, started the innovative team approach in which a number of people come to a conference table or a coffee shop and create sermons and ways to keep communication insightful and stimulating.

American youth ministry needs to keep paid youth workers from burnout, and one way is to enlarge the team of communicators. Add a few volunteers, parents, and a few *students* (more on student leadership and volunteers later). Consider for your team people who have computer graphic skills, musicians who coordinate the arts and worship, and detail people to make sure everyone is on the same page.

Some churches use the model that only one or two people have the gift of teaching, and I believe that is flawed and erroneous. There are many gifts in the body of Christ, and there are many who have the Spirit's power to communicate God's truth. There is more than just a rock star.

Add Small Groups and Two Leaders for Each One

Small groups (two to eight people) for students are great because they are not lecture driven, but each person has a chance to speak. It is important in youth ministry that teens relate to a number of adults *besides* the youth pastor. And for legal and child protective issues (some churches have a two-deep rule or safe-sanctuary policy), it is important that teens not be alone with an adult. Why have small groups with leaders other than the rock star pastor? Answer: It will take some of the stress and strain off the leader and lighten his or her load, and it is healthier for all involved. The pedestal is harder to find when others are doing ministry.

Let Students Process, Interact, and Debrief

One of the obvious ministerial pressure points and symbols for being on the pedestal is having to be the *expert*. It is understood in America that we have experts on every corner for every job in the workplace. We have specialists for everything. The problem is that it creates a false persona in ministry, not to mention that the Bible does not teach the spiritual gift of *expertise!*

What happens to the superstar youth worker who teaches all the time and then one day announces he or she is leaving? The church panics and kids start crying and threatening to leave when the new leader on the block isn't as dynamic or spiritual as the previous one. Oftentimes the ministry falls apart because the foundation was built on the shoulders of Superman or Wonder Woman.

The one-person show is not only unbiblical but also anti-biblical. One danger of the one-man or one-woman talking head is that it becomes toxic and unhealthy. And the gravest peril of all is that ministry becomes *personality driven.*

A plurality of teachers will help resolve some of the "who is speaking at the retreat" syndrome. Think communication without much lecture. Think "talk, debrief, and process."

Let me give an example of an experience I had—more of an experiment that I tried out to test my theory of learning. I was invited to speak to several hundred high school students recently in what I would consider a horrible teaching and learning environment—a church gym.

I told the youth pastor that it would be an interactive talk that would give the students time to contemplate the message, act on it, and share their discoveries. My message was from Genesis 37 and was about Joseph having a God-sized dream. I spoke maybe ten to fifteen minutes at the most. I gave each student a handout of my talk and a pen. I then directed that for the next twelve minutes each person was to go be alone with God and pray. My question was, "What big dream(s) has God put in your heart?" As music played in the background, the students took time to reflect and process. At the twelve-minute mark, I asked them to gather back together, and then for a few minutes each person shared with a small group the dreams God had given them.

Finally, as a symbol of closure with the community of faith, we had two standing microphones in which students could describe in thirty seconds to a minute what was on their heart and mind.

One by one students came and talked about their dreams. Some were small, some were medium size, and others were huge. I had to stop the sharing time after twenty minutes (it must be a Methodist thing to get out on time!).

It has been two months since I did the experiment, and there has been amazing feedback. Here is one Facebook comment to me: "Hey Dr. Olshine, I just wanted to let you know that, through one of your lessons, God saved my life. So thanks." Why was this student touched? My lesson did not save her; rather, it gave her and the other students freedom to debrief and process, and in the time of quiet reflection, this girl internalized the message. There is no need for rock star youth pastors when the body of Christ comes together to interact over what God's doing!

Use the Unsung Heroes (Parents) as Teachers

I am not sure where we came up with the model of keeping parents away from student ministry, but we need to involve parents as small-group leaders, speakers, Bible study leaders, and helpers.

I have lost count of the number of phenomenal parent helpers I have had over the years, but three in particular come to mind: Linda, Mavis, and Tom. None of these three came from a Bible college or were seminary trained, nor did any of them want to be "preachers." They are parents who walked the walk and talked the talk. All of their children agreed that they could be involved in the ministry. Sometimes we do have parents who want to be overly involved. One parent in one of my youth ministries wanted to help out with everything, but her daughter continually asked me *not* to have her involved, because she was very much a helicopter parent—strict and overprotective, one who hovered over her daughter and gave her little freedom or opportunity to succeed (or fail) on her own. The crisis escalated to the point where I had to ask her to back off in our youth ministry until she and her daughter worked out their angst.

Linda, Mavis, and Tom were not there to criticize, spy on their kids, micromanage their children, or gossip about the youth pastor. They were in youth ministry to serve, and thankfully their children wanted them to be present.

Linda, Mavis, and Tom have a heart for Jesus, love the word of God, and are called to work with students and families. They have given themselves to their families first and to the church second. Linda, Mavis, and Tom believe their first ministry is to their own family, and then they pour their lives into teenagers who are churched or unchurched.

Partner with parents. Allow them to use their gifts. It will reduce pedestal time for the fatal attraction of being the rock star youth leader.

Some Ministries Need to Add Paid Staff

One of the earliest guidelines in youth ministry still seems practical to me: one paid youth worker hired for every fifty students. It takes enormous time and energy to lead and shepherd fifty students. So if the group grows to one hundred, it only makes sense to add another staff person. I have observed over the years in my own ministry that if middle school ministry is staffed with the right leader, the group will grow because those in junior high still haven't hit the "cool factor" and aren't as quick to shy away from inviting their friends to youth group.

In my second youth ministry, I was the director of youth and young adult ministries with more than four hundred students in attendance. I was a hands-on leader with ninth-grade through twelfth-grade teens (senior high). Besides me, our team included these positions:

- high school programmer (thirty hours per week)

- middle school minister (full-time)

- administrative assistant (full-time)

- college pastor (full-time)

- two year-round college interns (each at fifteen hours per week)

- five full-time summer college interns

- two juniors or seniors in high school doing ministry weekly at $50 each

I am not suggesting that hiring more people will totally alleviate the pedestal problem, but it sure helps in eliminating some of the lead person's burden that is carried on a daily basis.

The paid person should be working himself or herself out of a job. There is an old axiom that states a fourfold process of giving away a job:

1. "I do it and you watch."

2. "I do it and let you help."

3. "You do it and I help."

4. "You do it and I watch and applaud."

It is arrogant and prideful for a youth leader to believe it's "all about me." The Bible says "pride goes before a fall," and God uses the foolish and the lowly. A refreshing perspective from a youth worker is when he or she can say, "I can do everything through Christ, who gives me strength," and "apart from [Christ] I can do nothing" (Philippians 4:13, NLT; John 15:5, NLT).

I will take a teachable, insecure, reluctant, and apprehensive youth worker any day of the week over a cocky "been there, done that" kind of leader. Find people to fill the gaping holes and enlarge their view of serving, then stand back and applaud every one of them!

Don't Build the Pedestal

Why build the pedestal anyway when we know that it will come down someday? Maybe it is because deep within each of us is a need for affirmation and approval and compliments. Working with people is exhausting and intimidating, and we do have critics around us, looking to tell us when we've dropped the ball. The bottom line is that most of us are insecure, and then we begin to think *I need to run to Walmart and buy game stuff and go hang out with a kid and then go study for my talk and...* ad nauseam.

Be like Nehemiah: look around the walls and see the damage, and then find some people who can carry the load with you. First Peter 2:5, 9 says, "You also, like living stones, are being built into a spiritual house to be a holy priesthood, offering spiritual sacrifices acceptable to God through Jesus Christ.... But you are a chosen people, a royal priesthood, a holy nation, a people belonging to God, that you may declare the praises of him who called you out of darkness into his wonderful light."

The Bible speaks of every Christian as a "priest" or, for our understanding, a "minister." All Christians are ministers. This is a radical concept for some people. Every follower of Jesus has been called to what the Reformers referred to as "the priesthood of all believers."

The priesthood is a reference to the books of Exodus and Leviticus, in which the priests went before God on behalf of the people. They prayed and taught and preached and served. The implication is that in the church we have professionals and paid clergy who do ministry, but we also train the "laity" to serve in their areas of giftedness. In fact, most paid clergy and church professionals were at one time volunteers who caught a passion and calling from Jesus to make a greater impact, so they headed for more education.

The person who says, "We hired you to do all the work," has never comprehended Peter's first epistle. All believers and disciples of Jesus are royal priests who can teach and lead and serve and minister in the name of Jesus.

Give as many jobs away as you can, and make sure people are trained and supported.

Voices from the Trenches

"It starts with the church leadership praying and discerning the youth pastor's job description. It must be clear that we are not hiring a 'one-person show' but a leader of leaders. The youth pastor must have the capacity to train both volunteers and students by putting them in places of leadership. Certainly the youth pastor needs a certain upfront vision-casting role, but he or she does not need to be the center of attention. The rock stars are the youth, not the youth pastor."

—Jeff, pastor of local outreach

Do Less, Delegate More

When paid youth staff comes out of the gate as in a race, many of them interpret ministry to be like a 100-yard dash—fast and explosive. *I know I did.* But something happens over time: we realize that we do a *few things well* and have been trying to do too much. All of a sudden we recognize this is not a sprint, nor is it about speed; it's about pacing and endurance. We are running a marathon.

The less we do, the more effective, sustainable, and efficient we will be. And the adage is true here: do less, and delegate more. I have found out that as I get older, I am able to fine-tune my gifts. I am gifted in four areas: communicating, discipleship, leadership consulting, and counseling. In other areas I'm pretty deficient.

If I focus on my few areas of giftedness, everyone wins. The opposite is also true: the more I do in ministry, the less others will do. If I want to create a culture of spectators, then I need to do as much as possible on my own. However, if I want to stir up a community of participants, I need to delegate more and do less. Then the pedestal is no longer wanted or needed.

Voices from the Trenches

"Avoiding the allurement of the four 'P' words can keep a young youth minister in check: program, performance, production, and personality. If you find yourself caught in the mode of centering everything on your personality, your programs, your production value, and your performance, your ministry will be ineffective and you will become another youth ministry statistic and casualty."

—Andy, bi-vocational worker in the church and marketplace

Overprogramming Feeds the Messianic Complex—Slow Down!

One youth pastor, Nathan, told me, "I enjoy being the star of the show sometimes. I like being needed. In fact, I am wondering if I went into student ministry because I *needed* to be needed." He continued, "I hate to admit it, but sometimes I like being called late at night to be superman in a crisis. I thrive on the idea of teens admiring me, parents praising me, and my community sending kudos my way. My head started to get big, way too big."

Nathan continued: "I started believing in a false way that I was Messiah-like and that I could really fix people. *It got out of control.* I became the center stage; I was a ministry addict and the church was my mistress. I was obsessed with 'me' and doing ministry. I had trouble delegating and found myself getting angry all the time. In fact, I began seeing a Christian therapist my last year of church ministry. One day he asked me a series of questions, such as: 'Why are you so angry?' and 'Did you go into ministry angry, or did the ministry create the anger?' and 'What are you really angry about?'"

After months of counseling, Nathan came to the conclusion that he was tired of being a superstar: "One night I fell apart, sobbing on the couch with my wife. She was totally supportive. She asked me, 'Honey, what do you want to do?' I decided to put the superstar out of his misery. I buried superman and put him out of his pathetic misery. I told my pastor and elders two days later that I was finished. The ministry needed to go on without me. My soul had nothing more to give. I was dried up, and the superstar in me was done."

Voices from the Trenches

"The overall vision for the position of a youth pastor for the American church must change. Unfortunately, many churches have adopted the image that if you get just the right person with a dynamic personality—one who can give an emotional talk and can plan events that will draw huge crowds—you have the right person in place.

"The idea must shift from a ministry that revolves around one person to a team-building ministry that is leveraging resources to impact young people and their families. The best protection a church can have for a youth worker is refining its vision for the position of youth worker, a vision that isn't based on producing numbers at all costs but is about building a community of believers who are willing to invest in the lives of teens, not just one person on a solo mission."

—Brent, paid youth worker

Q's to Enlarge

1. What are some practical ways in which you can get rid of the pedestal?

2. How can you ensure that your church or organization doesn't head down the road of rock star ministry?

3. Who are some people whom you can trust to help carry the load?

Chapter Four

WHAT ARE WE TRYING TO DO?

"We pay you to stay busy and keep the kids active."
—comment from a senior pastor to his paid youth leader

A knock on my office door changed my life.

I didn't know the man who introduced himself as "Kent." I was the new youth pastor on the block, and Kent was concerned about his new stepson named Matt, who was nowhere on my radar since I had only been working at the church for several months.

"David, can you fix Matt up?" he asked.

"What do you mean?" I inquired.

Kent described how Matt was a loner and viewed as an outcast at school, tried his skills on the wrestling team, and yet had lost every match so far. Matt had few friends at school, was bored with life, and, much to the chagrin of Kent and his wife, had no interest in God or church. Kent invited me over for a meal.

Two weeks later my wife, Rhonda, and I went over for dinner with Matt and his family, and it was awkward! Matt was such an introvert that he mostly grunted through dinner. Following dessert, I asked him if he wanted to go outside and shoot some hoops.

It was one of the longest twenty minutes of my life. Matt was a lost soul, and I was not going to be able to help him. I told Rhonda on the way home, "Thank God I will not have to see him again."

Wrong.

Matt started showing up to youth group (without any invitation from me) and then attended the backward progressive dinner (a fun event in which you start in one home with dessert and progress backward through the normal courses of a meal, finishing up with snacks). To my surprise, when it was time to sign up for our first-ever mission trip, Matt's name was on the list. It was on that trip that Matt gave his life to Jesus while hiding under a minivan. That's right, a church van. I will explain later. I spent three more years with Matt, teaching him how to pray and read the Bible and how to connect with his family and friends. Matt headed to college and then onto seminary, and today Matt is serving Jesus in a church, ministering to families and teenagers.

What's the point? I almost missed reaching out to Matt.

What's the Problem?

American youth ministry is a bit lost. It happens easily.

I once heard the saying, "If you aim at nothing, you are guaranteed to hit it every time." Youth ministry could learn from this concept because we are in a rut.

I am convinced American youth ministry doesn't know its primary purpose: making disciples.

When Kent knocked on the door, it altered how I would do ministry the rest of my life because otherwise I would have never invested in Matt's life.

If not for his concerned stepdad, Matt would perhaps never have been sought after and found. Kent knew that he needed other voices in Matt's life, and Kent had done as much as he could.

Sometimes parents' voices are silenced by their kids.

And instead of doing all we can to make disciples of teens and families, we end up creating lots of movement without much *momentum*. We start looking and acting more like a YMCA with events and ministries without many disciples.

Somewhere in time the American church drifted from making disciples of Jesus to talking about "accepting Christ," a phrase not found in the Bible. This drift has slowly started eroding the soil of American youth ministry.

I hear comments like these after summer camp:

- "Sixty-two kids accepted Christ."

- "Several of our students made significant steps for Jesus."

- "One of my students is going into full-time Christian work."

- "Billy prayed the sinner's prayer."

Now, don't get me wrong. I celebrate and rejoice over these kinds of commitments and life-changing decisions when it comes to following Jesus. The problem that surfaces in our day and age is this: one can be a "believer" in Jesus and not be a disciple of Jesus. You cannot be a disciple without believing—it's impossible. Believers hold to certain creeds and beliefs and teachings and doctrines. That is what a believer is all about—believing. A disciple, however, does more than just believe, a disciple follows and imitates Jesus.

Can one be a believer in Jesus without ever becoming a disciple? Yes. Our goal, however, is to produce disciples, not just believers.

Jesus Calling

The calling of Jesus when he started his ministry at around thirty years old was to make disciples. He chose twelve men to follow him, and his method was to transform them into world changers. In Mark 3:14 we read that following an all-night prayer meeting with his heavenly Father, Jesus called them "that they might be with him and that he might send them out to preach." Notice the progression: Jesus wanted to be *with them* and then later would send them out. Much of the disciple-making process is *relational*. Many youth workers do an exceptional job in the relational area of life. Some theologians refer to this as incarnational ministry—that Jesus came from heaven to earth, going from fully God to a human being who "moved into the neighborhood" (John 1:14, *The Message*).

We in youth ministry must do the same.

If we youth workers are committed to becoming disciples of Jesus ourselves, then we must not only say what the Rabbi says and do what the Rabbi does but also follow his methodology of ministry.

Too often American youth ministry tends to look to cultural rather than biblical ways to navigate the process when it comes to reaching people, and few seem to be asking the question, "What are we trying to do?"

Problem #4 of American Youth Ministry:
Our models of ministry and methods lack intentionality and end up being non-sustainable.

Imagine this case scenario: the church staff gathers around a long table on a Tuesday for a staff meeting. Each person has about two minutes to explain what is going on in his or her particular ministry. The meeting opens with praying for the sick of the church, and then each paid leader checks in with a short report.

Children's director: "We are getting geared up for our Halloween festival, and we need twenty-five more volunteers to help."

Executive pastor: "There have been some unlocked doors in the building, and I need everyone to please not give out keys to people who aren't on paid staff."

Youth minister: "We have a Messy Game Day coming up this Saturday, and then next week we are going to the Braves baseball games…and the van is broken down."

Adult education minister: "We are trying to start some new Sunday school classes for adults, but nobody is stepping up."

Senior pastor: "We had two people join the church."

Secretary: "Pastor, your sermon yesterday lasted thirty-four minutes."

Custodian: "The bathrooms on the third floor have been stopped up, so please be patient until we fix them."

Okay, are you seeing what I'm seeing? Good intentions, some stabs at being relational, but where is even the slightest hint of discipleship? The art of discipleship is painfully missing. The church has lost its disciple-making edge. That is a huge problem. Youth ministry must get this one right!

I have a brilliant idea: let's go to the manufacturer's handbook (the Bible) to see how Jesus reached and connected with people in his day.

Finding a Solution

Jesus chose ordinary guys to follow him. Why this strategy? Jesus was modeling his method of reaching the world. In his seminal work, *Master Plan of Evangelism*, Dr. Robert Coleman points out that Jesus had no other plan to save the world than by pouring his life into these men. Seems like a strange and bizarre way of reaching the world, hanging out with twelve guys for three and a half years. But it worked (and, might I add, still does). Jesus' final words following his death and resurrection were restated again: go make disciples.

So what's the problem? Our models of ministry and methods are oftentimes ineffective, nonintentional, and non-sustainable.

Look at how Jesus went about transforming the world: "Simon (to whom he gave the name Peter), James son of Zebedee and his brother John (to them he gave the name Boanerges, which means 'sons of thunder'), Andrew, Philip, Bartholomew, Matthew, Thomas, James son of Alphaeus, Thaddaeus, Simon the Zealot and Judas Iscariot, who betrayed him" (Mark 3:16-19, TNIV).

If you know any of these ragtag characters, you know they are not the elite of the elite. They were not popular or political. Simon Peter was a loudmouthed fisherman who exuded confidence and arrogance and insecurity. He ended up denying Jesus three times.

We don't know much about Alphaeus, Thaddaeus, or Simon the Zealot. Judas Iscariot betrayed Jesus after following him for three years and out of deep sadness and grief committed suicide by hanging himself.

Matthew was a hated tax collector, and Andrew was a Billy Graham–type evangelist in the making. My favorite disciples of the group are James and John, sons of Zebedee. I imagine Mr. and Mrs. Zebedee were thrilled when their two boys were called to leave the fishing industry and follow Rabbi Yeshua (see Matthew 4).

Sons of Thunder

Many people have an image of Jesus as constantly serious and focused, but in this passage of Mark 3, we see the humorous and lighter side of the God-man. He gives the boys a nickname, "sons of thunder."

Why did Jesus call them "sons of thunder"? There is a story behind the story told in Luke 9. The Jewish community of Jesus' day did not like the Samaritans or vice versa. Part of Jesus' mission was to extend his message to all people, Jews and Gentiles. Samaritans were somewhat different because they were half-breeds, part Jew and part Gentile. Part kosher and part ham sandwich.

Back to Luke 9. Jesus sent messengers to Samaria, and yet the Samaritans were not open to the message. This is where James and John come in: "Lord, do you want us to call fire down from heaven to destroy them?" (v. 54). Sons of thunder! "Blow them up, Lord" was their cry. Nice nickname. They wanted to blast and destroy the Samaritans.

Jesus' response? "But Jesus turned and rebuked them" (Luke 9:55). Don't you like the fact that two of the twelve people Jesus chose to change the course of the world were impulsive hotheads?

The disciples of choice were imperfect people. Later we know that the same sons of thunder became disciples of love. John would end up writing the Gospel of John; First, Second, and Third John; and the Book of Revelation.

Legend has it as John the Beloved was old and dying, his followers wanted to hear one final word of wisdom from the former son of thunder. "Love one another," John said. Then he became quiet. "Is there more?" someone asked. "No, that is enough."[1]

Solution to Expect:

Get back to the heart of Jesus' mandate of discipleship.

What are some keys for us to get back to Jesus' mandate? I'm so glad you asked. For the bulk of the chapter, let's talk about ten practical ways to implement discipleship to this generation.

Voices from the Trenches

"It's easy to fall into the temptation of focusing on producing numbers. We feel this pressure for hitting numbers from our church members and pastoral leaders. The problem with embracing this temptation is we lose sight of what truly produces lasting change in a kid's life, which is intentional discipleship. Jesus did ministry with the masses, but he focused much of his attention on three disciples (Peter, James, and John). Disciple-making can be difficult, but we can't let it fall by the wayside if we are going to be successful in youth ministry."

—Brent, paid youth worker

---

1. Does the Church Have a Mission Statement That Involves Discipleship?

Today it's trendy and in vogue for churches to have mission statements. Does your congregation have one? If so, what is it, and why is having a mission statement vital? If your organization does not have one, get a team together and create an exciting one.

A mission statement tells you where you are heading. A mission statement tells you what you are about, your values, and what gets your heart beating. In my opinion, most youth ministry mission statements are nonexhilarating and downright boring.

If you have a declared mission statement that includes the words *disciple, discipleship,* or *getting to know Jesus,* ask your team how you will go about achieving it. Some churches talk a good game about discipleship but have no idea how to "get 'er done."

What would be Jesus' mission statement? He modeled it for over three years, and his final words following his death and resurrection sealed the deal: "Go and make disciples."

I find it interesting, disturbing, and alarming that most church mission statements don't resemble anything close to having the phrase *making disciples* in it. I find it fascinating that a person's last words are something that are intended to "stick" and be embraced. Jesus' last words were not:

- "Go build buildings."

- "Go start big rallies."

- "Go and hide away this message."

- "Go start edgy programs."

Nope. None of these.

There is a recent trend of some youth ministries to break away from the language of the church's mission statement to create their own. Some like this and others don't. I personally feel that a youth ministry mission statement needs to reflect the "big church's" focus, but what happens when the "big church" does not have ownership to discipleship?

Time to call an audible.

2. Does Your Youth Ministry Have a Compatible Mission Statement?

I just finished consulting with a youth ministry that had no mission statement. They were floundering and fraught. We took several days and nailed it down: "Leading students and families to be devoted disciples of Jesus and to radically change our community."

Fifteen words. That's it. Now the task is: what does this mean? What does it look like? How do we get there?

In her book *The Path*, Laurie Beth Jones says that no one will remember a mission statement if it's too wordy. She suggests three ingredients to a great statement:

- It should be no more than a sentence long.

- It can be recited by memory at gunpoint.

- It can be understood by a twelve-year-old.[2]

3. Be Intentional on Mentoring and Coaching Volunteers, Parents, and Students

If your mission statement only mentions working with teenagers, think again about what the purpose of your ministry is to call parents, volunteers, and students into discipleship. If your mission statement excludes parents and volunteers, I suggest that you consider tweaking it. Start small.

If you are a parent, wouldn't you be happy to drop your kid off at church if its mission statement said, "We don't really want to put any pressure on parents so if you drop your students off to youth group frequently, we will train and equip them in the Bible and prayer and you can stay at home and watch TV."

I'm in!

But that is not what we want to communicate, is it?

Begin like Jesus with prayer (Luke 11) and ask him for a set of names to invest into. Consider three groups:

- parents

- adult volunteers

- students

I think discipleship should be creative and embryonic and have a grassroots feel to it. Be intentional, or you will quickly discover that other important ministry tasks will overcome your mission.

4. Read Over the Gospels and Get a Vision of Jesus' Style of Disciple-Making

What was Jesus' mission on earth? As a trained rabbi, Jesus spent three years pouring his life into twelve men who would turn the world upside down. It seemed like a slow and unexciting process. He lived and breathed his life with these guys. One was a fisherman named Peter who would later deny Jesus; Thomas was a doubter and skeptic; two were brothers nicknamed "the thunder brothers"; and Judas turned out to be a traitor and committed suicide. None of the disciples were great or powerful; most were poor and some illiterate.

Discipleship is personal. Jesus got up close and personal with these guys and reproduced his life into their lives. Jesus' closing words after the resurrection in Matthew 28:18-20 were, "Go and make disciples of all nations."

Discipleship is intentional. Jesus' plan was plain and simple: make disciples. Transforming a person into a "little Christ" involves a selection process, time, patience, and trust. Jesus prayed all night before he chose them. As fully 100 percent God and 100 percent man, the human part of Jesus had to trust and risk and pray a lot!

Discipleship is frustrating and messy at times. Even after hanging out with Jesus for over three years, his followers still did not always get his stories, and most of them did not understand that he would die and rise from the dead. At times the disciples were clueless. Yet Jesus loved them to the end.

Discipleship is primarily transformational. The disciples of Jesus would alter the course of history! The time spent with Messiah Jesus wasn't just informational; rather the disciples would be altered in order to be change agents. The disciples would be the leaders of the early church. Most would be killed for their faith, going out of this world into the next as martyrs. For example, tradition suggests that Peter was crucified upside down because he was not worthy of dying the same kind of death Jesus experienced.

Read the Gospels and see how Jesus spent most of his time with potential world changers (the twelve). It will give you a vision of more intentional "hang time" with teenage and adult reproducers.

Discipleship trains; most programs entertain. Programs are great, but people change people's lives. Get a vision of how Jesus discipled the twelve, and then consider doing some copying and imitating the model and method.

5. Understand Developmental Issues of Teenage Discipleship

Youth workers are oftentimes coerced into being with certain students because either the senior pastor has heard a complaint from a disgruntled elder whose son has been misplaced in the church or some teenager is extremely needy.

For whatever the reason, very few of us youth leaders can connect with every type of teenager. I have always found that kids from a sports background or the party scene were easy to relate to, since that is part of my background and story. On the other side of the coin, I have rarely been able to relate well with country life and car lovers although I love Disney's *Cars* and *Cars 2*!

As a paid youth worker, I realized that some kids wanted to be with me because I carried the "badge" of leadership and some wanted me to disciple them because they thought I was cool. The plus side of my investment into the lives of teens was that a number of parents were enamored with a youth pastor pouring his life into their kids. The downside was that some kids and parents were mad at me because I wasn't spending time with their tribe, and others were jealous. That is why a healthy youth ministry team has all kinds and types of adults loving and leading teenagers.

Teenage discipleship is not about sermons or limited to Sunday church or youth group. It probably won't look like "adult" discipleship. I think we need to be sensitive to the fact that many students are just trying to figure out who they are before they seek to understand who God is. Therefore, I see four developmental categories as we explore what teenage discipleship looks like. View these as sequential stages towards spiritual maturity.

Stage 1: Teenage Seeker

Sheldon comes to youth group because his parents make him attend. He doesn't really want to be there, but there are a few cute girls he likes to hang with. Sheldon is not necessarily against Christianity, nor is he totally disinterested. He just doesn't know what it's all about. He attends some events (which is a good thing) and appears to be open-minded.

Stage 2: Adolescent Affiliation

Allison loves coming to church and youth group for one primary reason: friendships. This is really normative for most students. Allison really does not know what she believes and would have trouble finding anything in the Bible. She is okay with that as long as she has her friendships.

Stage 3: Clinging To or Letting Go of My Parents' Faith

Hank cannot remember a time when he did not know Jesus and has been in church his entire life. Hank is starting to experience some doubts and questions about the Christian faith and is wondering if the faith his parents passed down to him is really worth trusting and believing in.

Stage 4: Teenage Ownership

JJ has been through ups and downs in his faith and is seeking with all his might to "name and claim" that this is his faith for the long haul. JJ wants a faith that is alive and lasts. He is starting to show signs of growth for himself and a concern for others to know and experience God. He is learning the Bible, is concerned about justice issues, and is starting to reach out to non-Christian friends at school.

Be aware: *Adolescent developmental issues play a huge role in faith development.* Sometimes I think we expect teens to have "adultlike faith," but in reality faith development takes time and must go through seasons of change, just like in the ecosystem.

In light of these categories, ask yourself these questions:

- "Am I expecting *too much* out of this person based on where he or she is developmentally, or am I expecting *too little?*"

- "Am I placing unrealistic expectations on these students? Am I allowing them to be kids?"

- "Am I challenging them with real biblical conviction or false guilt?"

- "Is this teenager really ready to share his or her faith, or am I imposing on him or her my lack of spirituality from when I was a teenager?"

6. Put Structures in Place So That All Students Will Be Cared For

In the Scriptures there seem to be four models of investing and discipleship. First, discipleship was from parent to child (which we discussed in chapter one). Second, discipleship embodies from an older mentor to younger, like women and men in the church. The letter to Titus states this model: "Teach the older men to be temperate.... Likewise, teach the older women to be reverent.... Then they can train the younger women.... Similarily, encourage the young men to be self-controlled" (2:2-6).

The third model was peer to peer (the twelve disciples to each other) or Barnabas to Paul. Finally, the fourth model is the reproduction model: Paul to Timothy and Timothy to younger men.

To flesh this out in a busy culture is complicated because it involves meeting with others for a season (months to years). My advice is to find the structures and systems that work for your context and ministry.

Offer Small Groups

- Offer different small groups for seekers, believers, and leaders. Offer some small groups that are more "prayer and share" and others for "study and application." Some small groups should be geographically based (where people live), and others can be more "campus driven" (where people attend church or school).

- Some small groups should be "leader picks students." This is when two adults choose some kids to meet with during the week.

- Some small groups should be "students pick the leader." Have a list of what groups are being offered and who is leading. Encourage the kids to pick. For example: you publicize that there are two guy groups for freshmen guys. Eric and Terry are leading an "adventure wilderness" small group weekly, and Sam and Jesse are leading a study on dating and relationships. Allow the students to select which one best suits their needs at the time.

Visit Middle and High School Campuses

One of the most strategic ways to "connect with the fish" is visiting the middle and high school campuses. Please understand that many public and private schools have strict policies about evangelism on campus, so be respectful of their guidelines. I have found that if a school will allow me to come onto the property to have lunch with one of my students, I usually have to sign in at the office, fill out some waiver form, and wear a name tag.

Other schools will not allow visitors unless you have been screened by the principal or some authority from the school system. Some schools will allow youth workers to volunteer in various roles. For four years I served as the football chaplain at Colerain High School in Cincinnati. I have spoken in classes and school assemblies.

If you want to get onto the school campus, find out the protocol. Look at the school calendar to see what events you can attend. Gaining a presence on campus is a great way to start the process of incarnational ministry and discipleship.

7. Understand the Selection and Multiplication Process

Picture yourself at the grocery store in the fruit or vegetable section. Your spouse wants a watermelon, cantaloupe, and grapes. You just aren't sure if they are ripe and ready for the taking, so you shake and smell each one. It is hard to know which one to select. It is the same when it comes to selecting students to invest one's life into for discipleship.

To be totally honest, I have chosen teens for discipleship who ended up doing great things for God, and I have also had kids who looked like a spiritual giant-in-the-making but walked away from Jesus (like Demas, who is mentioned in 2 Timothy 4:10).

In order to understand the selection process, Jesus modeled discipleship with the starting point: *prayer.* Pray for the right persons to invest in (Jesus prayed all night): "God, who do you want me to pour my life into who might be ripe enough to reproduce and multiply into other people?"

Discipleship is based on the concept of multiplication. This multiplication is explained by the Apostle Paul in 2 Timothy 2:2: "And the things you have heard me say in the presence of many witnesses entrust to reliable people who will also be qualified to teach others." Notice the process: Paul invests his life into Timothy, who proceeds to pour his life into reliable people who in turn impact and teach others.

I would like to give you a definition of *discipleship: the process of a Christ-follower investing, pouring, modeling, mentoring, and reproducing his or her life into the life of another.* We need to become intentional at making disciples. Jesus died for this to become "normal Christianity." Jesus specifically spoke of discipleship; the American church speaks about believing in Jesus. Let's get this right and get back to the heart of making disciples, not just believers.

8. Real Discipleship Precedes Evangelism in Youth Ministry, Not the Other Way Around

Most American churches seem to have a formula that I daresay hasn't worked well. It looks like this: teach and nurture and teach and nurture and then ask them to commit to Jesus and then hope they turn out fully mature disciples. We encourage people to "pray the sinner's prayer" by standing up or raising their hand, and then usually we tell the "new convert" to start attending classes and Bible studies. Eventually these young believers will grow up and be really mature, or so we hope.

In reality, *discipleship precedes evangelism best in youth ministry.* When I use the term *discipleship* here I mean the process of intentionally relating and connecting to a student for a period of time during which trust and communication are built. It is exactly what Jesus did when he started his three-and-a-half-year adventure with the twelve apprentices. When you look at Jesus' ministry, you see that he spent most of his time with the twelve disciples. Why? Because his training method was for one purpose, as described in Acts 17:6: "These [men] who have *turned the world upside down* have come here too" (NKJV; emphasis mine)

As we spend lots of time with students, we earn the right to be heard and trusted. We disciple and then lead them, every step of the way, into a relationship with Jesus—and never stop. Rather than praying the prayer and wishing the person desires spiritual growth, the discipleship model looks like this:

Discipleship_____Evangelism_____More Discipleship

Here's a real-life example I had with a junior named JB. I was the chaplain of the high school football team, and he did not have a church background at all. He was on the football team, and on Friday mornings we had a meal and short Bible study. He attended our "breakfast club" weekly. I started to hang out with JB (relational discipleship) and his friends who happened to be in my youth group.

I asked JB to be in my Bible study on Wednesdays after football practice, and he agreed. I continued to pour my life into him, and one afternoon JB said he wanted to start a relationship with Jesus. JB took that big step of faith to receive Jesus. Notice, though, the process did not stop. My Bible study group of guys kept leading him more and more into Jesus, teaching and training JB in the basics of the faith: reading and applying the Bible, how to study God's word, how to pray, and how to share one's faith. The discipleship pattern never stops. Today JB is a church planter in the Midwest and is multiplying his faith into others.

9. Create Rites of Passage: Boys to Men

Around the time of Jesus' birth, Jewish males were reading and memorizing the Torah (the first five books of the Bible: Genesis, Exodus, Leviticus, Numbers, and Deuteronomy) at an early age. It was an honor to study Torah and teach it. Becoming a rabbi (teacher of the Law) was one of the greatest privileges, callings, and honors to receive.

Luke 2:42-51 records Jesus going to Jerusalem with his parents. Every adult male living within fifteen miles of Jerusalem was expected to attend the Passover festival. A Jewish boy became a man at twelve years old, so you can imagine the excitement Jesus must have been feeling while journeying to Jerusalem. This was certainly a rite of passage for him, or at least a taste of great things to come. When the Passover had ended, Mary and Joseph headed home, each thinking Jesus was with the other parent as they traveled separately in caravans.

When Mary and Joseph realized he wasn't with them, they returned to Jerusalem and found Jesus where one would expect a twelve-year-old male of his day to be: in the temple. What was Jesus doing? He was sitting "among the teachers [rabbis], listening to them and asking questions." What were the rabbis thinking? They were "all quite taken with him, impressed with the sharpness of his answers" (*The Message*).

At age thirteen, a Jewish boy became a bar mitzvah, a "son of the Law," in which he entered into full adulthood. After I became a follower of Jesus, I was struck by the lack of rites of passage, traditions, and rituals in the church I attended.

As a Jewish follower of Jesus, it dawned on me how much of the church in general lacked symbols for me to connect with as a young believer. A few years later, as a youth pastor, I observed that church was one of the last places a twelve-year-old male wanted to be!

Rather than constructing markers and models for teens to enter the life of the church body, we are stuck, lost in the maze, and bumbling around trying to prevent a mass adolescent exit from the church. What seems to be missing is a rite of passage for teens, especially boys.

Why Boys?

It's not that we're leaving girls out. More girls seem to be naturally attracted to youth group and church than boys. Boys don't even seem to like church. Youth ministries need to find creative and innovative ways to reach boys. Adults (parents included) and adolescent boys are separated by a huge gulf, relationally speaking. There's an intergenerational disconnection between adults and teen boys.

On sabbatical a few years ago, I started researching rites of passage and boys. I interviewed people and sent out letters, voice mails, and e-mails, asking youth pastors and church leaders: "Do you offer any rites of passage for teenage boys?" The response was overwhelmingly "No." What was positive in these responses was the excitement of youth workers who wanted new rites of passage for male teens in the church. Yet the sad commentary came from a youth pastor in Illinois: "We don't do anything special for boys in the church, and we are losing them before they move on to high school. I have no idea what to do."

What Is a Rite?

The phrase *rite of passage* is far from new. The first book ever written on rites of passage was by Arnold Van Gennep in 1902, titled *The Rites of Passage* (Chicago: University of Chicago Press).

A rite of passage is a ritual that takes a person through a particular life cycle, such as baptism, first communion, and marriage; and yes, a funeral is a rite of passage. One must ask: "Do we have any rites of passage for American adolescence?" Some people might mention puberty; others say a teen's first sexual encounter. How about when an adolescent gets a driver's license and his or her first car? It seems that in our culture there are few if any rites of passage for teenagers. As one of my friends said, "Most children never know when they become adults."

What would a twenty-first-century rite of passage look like for boys? How do we produce a model of entrance rather than an exit ramp? Why not create a chapter in a male teenager's life in which he (like Jesus) listens, asks questions, and offers sharp answers?

Why Rites Are Meaningful

Rites are often bigger than us. They can be heroic, or a cause to be celebrated. Many would say marriage is a rite because it has the element of celebrating two lives coming together, becoming one flesh. In other words, marriage is bigger than one person. It affects not just individuals but the couple, parents, in-laws, friends, family, and neighbors. It's larger than life.

A rite of passage brings the star into a community experience. This passage is not to be done solo but is celebrated together with loved ones, family, and friends. It becomes a community event and involves a number of spectators and participants.

A rite is the beginning and ending. It marks the closure of an important time while signifying the beginning of another. With a contemporary bar/bat mitzvah, the community celebrates the individual. What are they dancing and clapping about? *The exiting of childhood, and the entering into adulthood.*

It's a spiritual experience. At the heart of Jewish bar/bat mitzvahs is the presence of God, and the center of the experience is the Scriptures. If we are to establish these kinds of rites in the church, we should emphasize the word of God as the central theme for young men to honor and love.

The R.I.T.E. Approach

Before launching new rites of passage in your ministries, consider first the R.I.T.E. approach.

Read. Start reading about rites of passage. It's too easy for us to hear a concept and, rather than search it out, to start planning a meeting or an event. Resist doing anything until you start reading about ministry to teenage boys. Read before doing anything else, let it slowly simmer, and then allow it to boil.

Investigate. Some of the current church models, whether effective or impaired, happen in the forms of church membership or confirmation. In my first youth ministry, I was asked to lead a confirmation class, which was a foreign concept to me. Our church started a seven-week class for seventh-graders and then closed with a weekend retreat. It was a good experience for me and for them, with the exception of two boys, Ben and Ted, who told me they were *made* to do it by their parents. I asked them if they ever intended to come back to youth group and church, and both told me no. I asked why, and they said, "Church is boring."

A youth pastor from British Columbia told me recently, "We have tried to reach boys over the years, but nothing seems to fit quite right." He is not alone. Investigate what has and hasn't worked. Talk with people. Network. Ask what they're doing to connect with boys. Try to discover why something works or doesn't.

Target. Tim works with middle schoolers. He struggled for years about how to reach and keep boys. He developed a strategy of service projects as a motivational tool to involve and give ownership. Each year, these boys move up the ladder of servanthood. By the end of their middle school years, they will have served locally, statewide, and nationally. In their high school years, they are able to take more adventurous trips to Mexico and Central America. If they make it all the way through, there's a graduation trip before college.

Eric takes seventh- though ninth-grade boys on a seventy-two-hour backpacking experience with all sorts of experiential learning opportunities, and adult mentors come along to help lead small groups and team initiatives such as hiking and ropes courses. Eric wants to mold his boys from "wimps to warriors. I want them to sweat and love it."

Andrea and her husband are doing a type of bar mitzvah ceremony in which their son will take a purity vow along with other elements of deepening his life in God.

These are examples of people who have read, investigated, and determined their target accordingly. Without taking the first two steps, the target stage most likely will fail. So don't be impulsive or discouraged! Be patient, because this is a process.

Evaluate. We often skip this last step. Are we hitting or missing the mark? As you venture into new areas with teenage boys, test their fruitfulness. Ask some hard questions, such as:

- "Is this program working? Why or why not?"

- "What are the strengths and weaknesses of this rite of passage model?"

- "Are lives being changed?"

- "Do I have a good model?"

- "Are mentors involved? Parents? The church?"

- "Are teens more connected with the local church?"

- "Are students becoming more faithful disciples as a result?"

When it is all said and done, ministry to teenage boys is tough but worth it. There is much work to do in this area. May God lead us to new blueprints and systems with teenage males. Who knows, maybe you will be used by God to build the R.I.T.E. stuff for a new generation of men.[3]

10. Look for the "Under the Minivan" Moments

I began the chapter telling you about Matt, a quiet and introspective kid, kind of nerdy, and lacking social skills. When Matt came on our mission trip, little did I know that he had a deep-seated phobia: storms.

One night we were eating seafood as a team, and CNN mentioned a hurricane was heading to the part of the coast where we were working. So I told our group of students and adults to pile into the van and that we'd head to safety. As we were ready to leave the restaurant, Matt was missing. He was not on the van and nowhere to be seen.

I started shouting, "Matt, Matt, where are you?"

Then I heard a soft voice coming from underneath the minivan, "I am here." On the ground, hiding under the van, was Matt.

"What are you doing under there?" I asked.

"I am scared," he said.

"Of what?" I asked.

"Storms."

"Come out, Matt."

"I cannot, I am scared."

"Matt, if you don't come out, I swear I am going to run you over." (Just joking, but it was tempting!)

He came out, and we made it to back to our ministry site. Under the minivan Matt gave his life to Jesus.

God will grab people at their greatest place of need and often in the most unpredictable and strangest settings. There is no one right way to get people on the road to discipleship. Just look out for God to work in your students' lives—even under minivans.

Voices from the Trenches

"The American church has drifted from a biblical focus to caring about being too relevant. Relevancy matters, but it does not matter as much as making long-term disciples. If we take Jesus' instructions out of the church and youth ministry in particular, we are doomed to die. Anyone can draw a crowd, but it takes a humble leader to take the slow road of discipleship that leads to multiplication of world changers in the younger generations. This was Jesus' plan. It needs to be ours too."

—Jeff, pastor of local outreach

Q's to Expect

1. What structures are in place in your youth ministry for discipling students, volunteers, and families?

2. How are you doing with a mission statement that is discipleship driven?

3. What specific action steps do you need to take to make disciples so that they will make other disciples?

Notes

1. A. J. Conters, *The Eclipse of Heaven: The Loss of Transcendence and Its Effect on Modern Life* (Downers Grove: Intervarsity Press, 1992), 165.

2. Laurie Beth Jones, *The Path: Creating Your Mission Statement for Work and for Life* (New York: Hyperion Press, 1996), 3.

3. Portions of these comments were used by permission and taken from Youthworker Journal by David Olshine (http://www.youthworker.com/youth-ministry-resources-ideas/youth-ministry/11624004/).

Chapter Five

LET ME OFF THE RIDE!

"Toto, I don't think we're in Kansas anymore."
—Dorothy *in* The Wizard of Oz

I didn't know what I didn't know.

My dad took me to an amusement park when I was about six years old, and I begged him to take me on a Ferris wheel ride. It looked so easy from a spectator's view and it appeared that everyone on it was laughing and having a great time.

When it was my turn to get on, panic and anxiety came out of nowhere. My father assured me that it was no big deal and that I would have fun. As the metal handles came around me, I could feel my body getting tenser by the moment. The Ferris wheel began slowly and then accelerated to great speed and height. We went up higher and higher, and I started to tighten more, ready to throw up or wet my pants. Instead, I freaked. I started to scream, "Let me off this ride. Let me off this ride. Get me off!" The nice old man who operated the fine piece of machinery was compassionate enough to stop the ride.

Sometimes I think American youth ministry needs to stop the ride or at least slow it down.

What's the Problem?

Programs are events we utilize in youth ministry to build momentum, create excitement about spiritual things, build community cohesiveness, and reach out to seekers and lost students. When it comes to programming, the problem is that in most parts of the country American youth ministry has become obsessive and gone overboard.

72

We need to stop and ask ourselves the question, "What are we doing?" Some churches have gone manic, and organizations that become program driven hire more staff for the primary reason of creating more programs, which then leads to needing more help, which leads to bigger budgets and more stuff.

Seems to me like we have too much of "more stuff."

Problem #5 of American Youth Ministry:

Maddening program obsession.

Bart was minister of youth and young adults at the mega-church of First Church of the Burning Bush. He had five hundred–plus teenagers who were coming weekly. The job description for the student ministry is listed in the following order:

- Oversee the weekly Sunday school program (fifty-two Sundays a year) for sixth through twelfth grade.

- Organize fifty-two weekly Sunday night programs for sixth through twelfth grade (including Easter, Christmas, July 4th, Father's Day, Mother's Day, Thanksgiving, and Super Bowl Sunday).

- Plan and lead twenty Wednesday nights in the fall semester and twenty Wednesday nights in the winter/spring semester.

- Plan four to six mission trips annually.

- Plan and lead four retreats annually for middle school and high school (two each).

- Coordinate twice-a-month weekend events (Friday or Saturday).

- Plan one lock-in per grade annually.

- Oversee small groups off-site (besides Wednesday nights).

- Have one day off weekly for youth staff.

- Be in the building from 8:00 a.m. to 5:00 p.m. on most days.

- Attend staff meetings on Wednesday mornings with the executive team.

- Attend youth staff weekly meetings.

- Oversee five interns.

- Collaborate with children's staff and college ministry staff.

- Plan and lead parents' information meetings twice a year.

- Equip parents with two seminars per year

Are you tired yet? On top of that, Bart created a parents' advisory team that helped him discover that youth ministry was busy *296* days of the year.

Finding a Solution

If the bottom line of your youth ministry is the number of people attending, then perhaps your goals are skewed. I would agree that numbers are important because numbers are about people and people matter to God; plus, numbers give an indication of the pulse of the ministry. I think we need to also realize that in some places, bringing in an inspirational speaker and an awesome band can draw in a crowd but doesn't mean anything of significance was accomplished.

Consider these kinds of conversations that happen at youth worker conferences:

Scenario 1

Q: How was your year in youth ministry?

A: Great. Last year we had about thirty kids coming on Sunday nights and met in the church basement. This year we have grown to over three hundred and are moving into the civic center. We have thirty small groups with leaders and took four mission trips last year. Our calendar is full almost every day of the year.

Seems okay, right? I mean, we can celebrate the growth. Listen to the next discussion.

Scenario 2

Q: How was your year in youth ministry?

A: Great. We are discovering as a group what it means to follow Jesus and how to help our staff members be effective with students while maintaining good boundaries and sustainability. Our kids are learning how to make an impact in their schools, and we are doing some neat outreach to the poor. We are on a journey trying to figure out how to empower parents to influence their kids spiritually.

Do you notice any differences?

The first answer was primarily about *numbers effectiveness,* and the last response was about *growth and depth*—and attendance wasn't even mentioned.

Solution to Engage:
Program with purpose and stop worrying about numbers.

Before you can eliminate the madness, determine the reasons for program obsession. The key questions to ask are these: "What is the reason we obsess over the numbers of people who show up? And why does this become maddening for some?" There are a number of reasons for the obsessive madness of growing numbers in a group.

First is pressure from the top. I am all for reaching young people, but there are some senior pastors and leadership boards who place enormous pressure on youth workers to build attendance. I have been in both situations, in which I was pressured to grow a group and in which I mildly threatened the youth worker to get numbers or get another job. Maybe one of the elders or some committee member is unhappy with the fact that his or her child doesn't like youth group and wants to go to another church or Fellowship of Christian Athletes. I have seen students leave because a boyfriend or girlfriend goes to another church and Mom or Dad, who sits on the administrative board, is furious. This stuff happens every day.

Second, our self-worth is often tied into numbers and growth. In my opinion people in ministry generally have two qualities that are in the "crash zone." These manifestations are often in tension with each other: *drivenness* and *insecurity*. Part of our personality is drive: the drive to succeed and to impact and influence and make a difference in the world. This drive is in our DNA, and I am convinced God put it inside of us. The other side of the tension is insecurity. This part of our wiring deals with comparing ourselves with others, wanting to win teenagers to Christ, and fearing failure. The insecurity grows when other churches have better facilities or more cash flow or multiple staff positions. The youth worker sees that the national youth conferences only tend to invite speakers who have large and mega-large ministries, and before you know it, this leads to insecurity and sometimes a defeated attitude.

Third, numbers represent names and faces. Numbers do matter because numbers represent people and are indicators of movement (sometimes good, other times bad). Jesus told the parables of the shepherd and lost sheep, the lost coin, and the lost son in Luke 15. The story of the shepherd has incredible implications for those of us who work with students and families because by our very nature and calling, *we are shepherds.*

Jesus said, "Suppose one of you had a hundred sheep and lost one. Wouldn't you leave the ninety-nine in the wilderness and go after the lost one until you found it?" (v. 4, *The Message*).

So let's bring it closer to home: you have one hundred students in your ministry and one teen stops coming. Jesus' message is clear: leave the ninety-nine and find the one. That one matters to God. We should care about people. Programs don't keep students involved; people keep students involved. Programs are only a means to an end, not an end in themselves. Unfortunately, in our busy culture there are youth workers who will not go after the one lost one in order to nurture those in attendance.

Acknowledge the Seasons before You Plan

Any healthy youth ministry will acknowledge certain ebbs and flows and highs and lows of the calendar year. One of the mistakes we make is neglecting the public school calendar. One of the biggest boneheaded blunders I made was to plan a youth retreat that was also the weekend of SAT testing. If I had only taken the time to contact the schools closely related to our church, I would have planned the retreat for another time.

Look at holidays, sporting events, fall break, spring break, and summer break. Try to avoid times during which family vacations are a priority. Youth ministry should consider shutting down a bit in May (graduation) and December (Christmas) and slow the pace. Before you add or cut, check out the season you are in.

For instance, I live in the South, where college football reigns supreme in the fall (September through November). Since Saturdays are the holy grail, we must be careful about what we organize and implement during that season.

Voices from the Trenches

"Being 'missional' seems like a daunting task for American youth groups. Fortunately, creating a culture of 'purpose' for any youth group just needs three key ingredients: passion, vision, and implementation.

"First, identify an adult or student who is passionate about programming with purpose. That passion will be the driving force behind getting others on board with you and spreading the contagious nature of excitement. Second, there must be a vision (or a goal): 'Where there is no vision, the people will perish' (Proverbs 29:18). Take time to hash out a specific, real goal or mission statement. It allows for direction for everyone involved. Finally, you must implement ideas, even if you're not sure they're possible."

—Kristina, paid youth worker

Reduce the Proliferation of Programming

It just seems American youth ministry is obsessed about events and programs. Doug Fields writes, "I think most ministries do too much and they would be healthier if they cut their program opportunities in half."[1]

Ever heard of this principle? Less is more.

People assume the key to growing a vibrant student ministry is to hire more staff. I have observed over the years of my ministry that hiring more staff to work with students *does not* guarantee more effective ministry. What a new hire usually promises is *more programs* and more programs oftentimes keeps parents out of the loop and keeps the budget running higher and higher. Then the begging begins for volunteers to step up to keep the machinery going. Is it any wonder that people start screaming, "Let me off this ride!"?

Program with Purpose

Why do you do what you do?

Consider the needs of your community. Programs are the stuff we do. Programs are usually neutral, and there is no assurance that a program will be great or will bomb, and only time will tell whether it will be sustainable or need to be buried. God has gifted the church with amazing creativity and gifted people to do extraordinary things for his kingdom. Not every church can meet all the needs, but just ask yourself: what could we be doing in these areas?

1. Special needs

2. The underprivileged and disenfranchised

3. Training fathers to lead

4. Reaching teenage boys

Voices from the Trenches

"We are a busy society with lots happening. This does not seem to slow us down in the local church. There is a small or sometimes direct influence to 'fill the calendar' with programs and events to keep everyone active. Without purpose in programming, we will miss the target and eventually burn out in ministry. We need just a few purposeful programs that connect with the overall church vision and to pour talent and treasure into them over time. Make adjustments along the way, and sometimes stop and start new ones, but be intentional."

—Jeff, pastor of local outreach

Think Archery

As a young man, I attended a sports camp in the north woods of Wisconsin for five summers. We were expected to participate in all the activities, so I tried my hand at archery, and I became decent at it. Anybody who knows archery understands the goal is to hit the target: bull's-eye!

American youth ministry has gotten logjammed and bogged down with way too much activity and not enough productivity. Every youth ministry needs to ask itself these questions:

• "What are we aiming at, and are we hitting the target?"

• "If discipleship of parents is the bull's-eye, how are doing? Hitting or missing?"

- "If the bull's-eye you are aiming for is reaching unchurched and lost teenagers, are you close to dead center or way off target?"

Do simple youth ministry. Think archery.

Create Core Values

A core value is another way of asking the question, "Why do we exist as an organization?" or "Why did God put us in this place and at this time to do something with great significance?" Although people have been super-hyped over the years about creating goals, objectives, and mission statements, most of them in my opinion have been *underwhelming. Core values should be something that are out of the box, inspirational, and humanly nonachievable without the help of the Holy Spirit.*

As a youth pastor, now professor, communicator, and consultant, I can tell you from my experience that most organizations, churches, and youth ministries *have not* figured out their core values. They do not know what they stand for or what they're seeking to achieve. If you are feeling that, you are not alone. Some ministries and organizations get messed up in this process by trying to come up with too many purposes and values, and then they get "lost in the sauce."

Voices from the Trenches

"Programming in the church oftentimes gets a bad rap. Many people say that ministry should be organic and that programming simply turns the church into a machine. I disagree. I contend that poor programming creates the cogs and treads of a ministry machine, while purposeful planning creates a sustainable, systematic, and structured ministry that is fertile for the Holy Spirit to work. As we surveyed our student ministry a few years ago, we recognized that although we stated that ministering to parents was essential, our programming did not represent that. So we started with a purpose. Our purpose was to resource parents to be the primary disciple makers of their students. Out of that came a simple three-step approach. Step one was a summer program called 'Understanding Your Teen.' We brought in speakers on various topics such as drugs and alcohol or bullying. Step

---

two was a fall in-house retreat for parents and students to enjoy playing, eating, and learning together. Step three was a monthly newsletter to parents with everything from reminders to youth culture updates. When you can identify your purpose clearly, you can program in such a way that everything you do is done with precision and the Holy Spirit has freedom to move."

—Trevor, paid youth worker

Establish Clarity: Do One Thing Great

In 2012, I bought a new cell phone made by Apple. I felt really significant for about four minutes because it had all the "bells and whistles," that is, until my friend told me a newer iPhone had just come out two weeks before. Dang it! There is a good chance that my new phone is already a dinosaur by the time this book gets fresh ink on the pages. Why? Apple is committed to doing one thing great. No telling what will be created in the next twenty-five to fifty years.

What do you think of when I mention brand names such as Wal-Mart, Target, Chick-fil-A, Lowes, Home Depot, and Coca-Cola? Answer: They all seem to have a specialty they are known for.

- Wal-Mart and Target are considered one-stop shopping places; you can buy just about anything there.

- Chick-fil-A doesn't do hamburgers; they do chicken.

- Lowes and Home Depot have one mission: to provide home-improvement products.

- Coca-Cola wants to refresh the world in mind, body, and spirit with their products.

What is your ministry about? Are you great at anything? What is your niche? How are you unique? Once you discover who you are and why you exist, go after it with great passion!

Ask the "What" Question after Asking "Why"

When an organization begins the process of programming with purpose, there are some essential questions to lift up once you have answered the "Why do we exist?" question. First is the question, "What?"

- What programs and events are we going to keep based on the question "Why do we exist?" (Do the current "programs" fit the mission or just crowd up the calendar and people's time?)

- What programs are most important based on the "Why do we exist?" question?

- Are there any programs that should be added to fit the core values? If so, what are they?

Bedside Baptist Church has identified the "why" as "empowering parents and teens to be growing disciples." The church leadership then took a hard look at the programs and recognized that 75 percent of the events on the calendar were obstacles to the core value, so they began to prune the programs to fit their values.

Voices from the Trenches

"Why is it tempting to put our time and energy into programming? I believe it is because we buy into the lie that 'if we build it, they will come.' Take the great ministry of Young Life. Their version of programming is 'weekly club.' If you have ever been to a Young Life club, you quickly realized they do quality programming, but programming isn't their main objective.

"Young Life's main objective is to go into youth culture and build relationships with teenagers in order to help them get to know Jesus. The Young Life club supports their goal of sharing the gospel, but the relationships they build with teenagers are the main focus. Programming should never be our end goal, but sadly it is where we spend most of our time, resources, and energy. If we are going to program with purpose, we must remember that the programs we create will eventually end. Kids will graduate from our ministries and move on, and honestly they will not remember most of our programs. What students will remember is the time that we invested in them relationally. Programming has its place in youth ministry, but we must remember that it should never be our final destination."

—Brent, paid youth worker

Final Steps: How and Who

The last step to ponder is the "How" and "Who" questions. How will we achieve the value? How will we get there? A healthy organization must answer the "How" question, but understand there is one more step.

The next question is "Who?" Who is responsible for the "how"? There usually needs to be a director or point person who oversees the operation. Head coaches are excellent at the vision of an organization, but they have people surrounding them working out the details.

The youth worker must ask, "Who is going to be responsible for outreach? Shepherding? Parenting? Counseling?" Each team member (paid or volunteer) should know his or her role and purpose in the "who" category, and hopefully that role is in his or her skill set and passions.

Last Step: Game Day Sheet

Isn't it fascinating what we can learn from CEOs of large companies and NFL and college football coaches' game plans? Have you ever noticed an offensive coordinator's large laminated game sheet? They have hundreds of plays available to run.

As a ministry dedicated to programming with purpose, make sure your team comes up with a game sheet that articulates the values (why, what, how, and who). This is your game day sheet. It should not be a long manual that simply looks nice on someone's shelf (yours) but rather a short and concise paper that explains the overview I have mentioned above.

The game sheet reviews the pertinent questions to keep in front of us all the time:

- Why do we do what we do?

- What are we aiming at?

- Why do we exist?

- What is the one great thing we do?

- What are we going to focus on?

- How will we get there?

- Who are the persons to help us get there?

A healthy youth ministry sets the stage for great programming with purpose. Follow the steps outlined in this chapter so you can overcome the maddening obsession with program. And just maybe you won't have to scream, "Let me off this ride!"

Voices from the Trenches

"The kingdom isn't growing if we don't program with a purpose. I've been a part of Fifth Quarter, a football after-party hosted at our church since freshman year. It was labeled as an alternative outlet for students to have fun without all the junk that comes with partying on Friday nights. The program was designed to get students to fall in love with Jesus by getting involved, but it started to become a party without purpose. This year, a group of students started up the 'Street Team.' We wear super cool shirts and go around to as many students as possible, getting the word out about Jesus and what our youth ministry is all about. We are renewing the purpose of a program to further the kingdom and I can't wait to see where Jesus takes it!"

—Madison, high school student

Q's to Engage

1. How many activities are you doing with purpose? What are they?

2. Are there some events you need to cut, and if so, who can help you pull it off?

3. What's the one great "program" your ministry does well?

Notes

1. Doug Fields, HomeWord Center for Youth and Family blog, February 27, 2012, http://www.dougfields.com/.

Chapter Six

VOLUNTEERS
MORE THAN A BODYGUARD

"I come to youth group week after week and still don't know what I am supposed to do."
—Donnie, a two-year youth ministry volunteer

I went to bed late one night and had a nightmare. I was teaching my youth group, and in my dream my volunteers were standing at the back of the room in bodyguard fashion, sort of uninvolved and passive. Then several students started to get silly, and before you know it, there was mass chaos in the room. I lost crowd control, and my volunteers did nothing; they just stood and watched me sweat and suffer while I tried to teach a Bible lesson.

Then I woke up in a deep sweat and realized my fantasy was reality.

What's the Problem?

I have heard some churches say they "are a teaching church," meaning that they want to teach the Bible with great insight and clarity. That is great, but where are the churches that are "training churches"?

Since its inception, the church has been volunteer driven and volunteer led. Volunteers are nonpaid servants. The word *volunteer* appears only one time in the Bible, in Psalm 110:3: "Your people shall be volunteers in the day of Your power" (NKJV).

The church started with nonpaid servants and this practice continues today throughout the globe. In fact, few organizations rely upon the willing sacrifice like the church. Hospitals, schools, and sports teams need volunteers, but no other group relies on volunteers like the church.

We need willing nonpaid workers, yet American youth ministry has failed miserably in training volunteers. Don't get me wrong, we have lots of great people who volunteer, and some of them are tremendous in what they do. We have solid chaperones, but let's face it, there are way too many adults who stand up against the back wall during most youth meetings and just stare. They were made for more than being bodyguards.

We have got to get this right.

Problem #6 of American Youth Ministry:
Our volunteer training is weak.

Finding a Solution

When I began student ministry someone told me I needed volunteers, but I wasn't sure what to look for and, even more strategically, I wasn't sure why I needed adult volunteers. After trying to go solo for some time, it didn't take long to realize that I needed an extra pair of hands and eyes to go to Kmart, pick up food for the retreat, call the coordinator of the mission project, organize the pool party and lake day, schedule parents' meetings, send out flyers, and so on.

I needed help.

I could not relate to all the various subcultures of students, and not every student was drawn to me or vice versa. I did not need someone who just breathed and could quote Bible passages. I needed passionate adults who wanted students to grow in their faith. I would need to coach and train adults to love Jesus more deeply and to love students.

Solution to Encourage:
Recruit and train to serve, not to stare.

Where does one start when it comes to training volunteers who serve, not stare? It begins with building a quality team.

Build a Team

We must begin by recognizing the biblical base of the team approach. Scripture refers to having people surrounding the ministry as "laity" and "saints." Ephesians 4:12-15 speaks to "equipping of the saints for the work of ministry" (NKJV). Equipping is a Greek concept meaning "to mend or heal." Lead pastors and youth workers were never meant to do it alone. Laurel needed Hardy, the Lone Ranger needed Tonto, and Jesus needed the twelve disciples.

Biblically grounded youth ministry must be team driven. Whenever I speak about leadership, someone always asks, "What's one of the first things to do when starting out new in ministry?" My response is, "Build a team." The team must be cohesive and have buy-in to the values of the organization and the mission of the ministry. The team must be healthy and open with one another, willing to support, care, and confront one another in Christlike fashion.

Voices from the Trenches

"Separating adults from teens won't work if you want effective discipleship. Modern youth ministry needs to connect several adults to teens for maximum impact."

—Sam, professor of youth ministry, family, and culture

Begin Slowly and Prayerfully

Some youth workers have told me, "There is no one willing to help out with the youth group," to which I respond, "How much time have you spent praying about this area of your ministry?" Since there is no "perfect" volunteer, paid youth leaders will naturally make mistakes when it comes to finding and recruiting these servant leaders. I decided early on in my twenties that I did not want many parents as volunteers, so I proceeded to choose "the young and the restless" (that is, college students).

I realized within a few months that college kids were full of zeal and passion, and yet their commitment to anything for the long haul was predictably pathetic. As I got older (and hopefully wiser) my learning curve changed, and I began to see parents as great complements and partners in ministry (and the "cool factor" that college kids had and parents normally *didn't* have was overrated!).

In my early years of youth ministry, I made plenty of poor decisions. For example, I would grab just about anyone to be on my team who had an interest in teenagers. My irritation level accelerated because I was going after people too quickly and impulsively and sometimes left God out of the equation. At some seasons of ministry I was not even sure I wanted volunteers, and because I am a slow learner, it finally dawned on me that a volunteer is a *nonpaid servant* with limited times and different expectations than I had as a paid person. The lesson to learn is: when going after volunteers to assist in ministry to youth, take it patiently, slowly, intentionally, and prayerfully.

Voices from the Trenches

"The glory all goes to God, but the center of ministry for the youth pastor is the youth. As a result, we need to recruit and train volunteers who grow in their passion to love kids. I believe God has those volunteers in every church, but the youth pastor, parent, and other volunteers' job is to harvest more to surround youth with love, care, and opportunities to grow closer to Jesus. A youth pastor's reach only extends so far, but with a host of 'in the game' volunteers, more youth can be reached."

—Jeff, pastor of local outreach

What Are the Criteria?

What are you looking for? Decide what you want and don't want in a volunteer. For example, some want or need a married couple or a single person in his or her thirties. I tend to think in terms of not types of people but rather needs, so the question becomes, "What kind of jobs do I need filled?"

A few years ago I started praying and dreaming of a newsletter specifically for parents in our youth ministry. One day someone knocked on my office door and introduced herself as Liz. She shared with me that her two boys were in our youth ministry and that she wanted to help in some way.

I said, "Great. What do you like to do?"

At that point, Liz started laying out all the things she disliked. "I don't want to make cookies and punch, and I don't want to drive kids places or teach small groups or attend retreats." (I started thinking, *She is a perfect candidate for another ministry in the church*).

"What are you good at, Liz?" I questioned.

She said, "Well, I was the editor of my high school yearbook, and in college I majored in journalism." Now we were talking! Liz became the answer to my prayer, coordinating our parent newsletter and writing articles.

She was amazing, and if I had based my assessment on a particular type of person, I may not have selected Liz.

When I started dating in college, I came up with my "dream list." For years I wondered why I could not find someone who fulfilled the list. Then my buddy Mark told me one day, "David, you need to throw your list away, plus you are not that great anyway." (Ouch!)

No matter what list you come up with, there is no volunteer who will fit a role perfectly.

Know the Good, Bad, and Excellent Ways to Recruit

Let's start with some bad (I have tried all of these, by the way), so please learn from my gaffes.

Bad (These are horrible ways to get people involved.)

1. Threaten to quit the youth ministry unless some people step up and serve. In other words, "guilt your congregation" into serving in youth ministry.

2. Make the job seem easy with little responsibility.

3. Talk about the super-spiritual kids and don't mention the students who struggle with pornography, eating disorders, drinking, and drugs.

4. Recruit through the church bulletin and website. This will guarantee to get some folk you don't want on your team.

5. Tell a potential volunteer that "the Lord put you on my heart and I think you would be a great volunteer and it won't take much of your time at all."

6. Mention a volunteer who said no and within a year mysteriously disappeared.

Good (These ideas have an upside and downside to recruiting.)

1. Ask your students for input on who would be a good volunteer. Teens have a deep intuition and awareness of adults who care about them.

2. Ask current paid staff who might be helpful and useful on the youth ministry team.

3. Solicit feedback from current adult volunteers regarding other possible adults to add to the team.

Excellent (These thoughts have the intent of training the right people.)

1. Pray fervently for a team of people, ask around, and then initiate a conversation with some of these people.

2. Invite them to attend one or two youth gatherings with no commitment other than showing up.

3. Meet one-on-one and discuss their gifts and interest in youth ministry.

4. Discover if the person wants to help, and then do a screening process with a spiritual gifts inventory, Myers-Briggs temperament test, and a background check (done for all team members).

5. Involve them, integrate them, and initiate them into your world of youth ministry. Make sure that volunteers know the responsibilities, the time commitment (hours), and length of service you are asking for (six months? one year?).

Voices from the Trenches

"My church leadership rarely thanked me for volunteering. It was sort of like they expected all members to serve (which we should), but an occasional word of affirmation really helps. I have found myself bitter toward our leaders because we work our tails off and get little encouragement. The teens, however, were great at telling me how much I meant to them."

—anonymous volunteer

What TEAMS to Look For

As I mentioned earlier, it is tough to find the "perfect person" to be on the team because no individual has all the gifts, skill sets, and personality traits to get the job done. But if push comes to shove, here are five traits I'm praying and looking for in a volunteer.

T = Teachable

I don't know about you, but I don't want an adult volunteer who is a know-it-all about students or the Bible. I want a humble and approachable person to be on the team and not someone who always has to be right. The Bible says "pride goes before destruction" and a nonteachable person is a proud person. It's only a matter of time before a fall will happen.

E = Encourager

The Bible speaks of Barnabas, "son of encouragement," as the primary person to win over the Apostle Paul when no one dared get near this former murderer-persecutor-turned Jesus follower (see Acts 11:25-30). If it had not been for Barnabas, we might not have a Paul who wrote most of the New Testament. People thrive on words of affirmation.

Working with adolescents is challenging enough for adults, and knowing that during the teenage years anxiety is at an all-time high, I want my team to be encouragers. I have never heard any student say, "I have had just too much encouragement today. No more, please!" On the real side of life, teens get more criticism than praise and need constant plugs, affirmations, and kudos from caring adults.

A = Authentic

I need my teammates to be real and authentic. Kids have built-in radar that we call "crap detectors," and students can spot hypocrisy a mile away. I want volunteers to be themselves—what you see is what you get. An adult who chooses to live a life of honesty, integrity, openness, and transparency in an appropriate manner will be loved and trusted by a teenager. A nonauthentic adult will not get the time of day from a student.

M = Maturity

I am aware that all human beings have problems, but wouldn't it be nice (and helpful) if our team ministering to the "now and next" generation came with little baggage! I want people on my team who have some maturity in their personhood—spiritually, intellectually, relationally, and emotionally. I don't need unforgiving people on my team or those who are constantly mad at the world or whine and complain all the time. I need some healthy people who love God, love themselves, and love others. I don't want needy people like Bob Wiley in the movie *What About Bob*, who runs to his therapist, Dr. Leo Marvin: "Gimme, gimme, gimme. I need, I need, I need."

S = Skill Sets (Sweet Spots)

The reality is, not every person on my team will be creative or energetic or funny, and I'm fine with that. But when I think of building effective teams, one thing stands out above the rest. I don't want people standing around doing nothing. That is a waste of their time and my time, and our students must wonder why the adults are hanging around the back of the room.

All teammates must come to the table with some skill set to help the ministry grow. When I played tennis in high school, my coach told us that there is a certain spot on a racket called the sweet spot. When I begin to identify jobs that are needed, I start looking for people to "flip the bill." In a face-to-face interview, I always ask, "What is your sweet spot? What gets you fired up?" Some of their answers might be

- Technology

- Set-up

- Tear-down

- Administration

- Music

- Food

- E-mails, flyers, and brochures

- Phone calls

- Graphics

- Showing movie clips/teaching slides

- Hosting team meetings in their home

- Teaching

- Leading small groups

- Setting up logistics

Then add to the list by answering these questions:

- What does our student ministry need?

- Where do I need help?

- What skills don't I have that others do and that the team needs?

Finally, I think it is vital that we recruit to our weaknesses, not our strengths. If a youth leader is weak at organization, then go find that person who ahs that gift. If you are a dreamer, you probably don't need many more visionaries. If you are finding yourself teaching all the time without much break, then go after some folk and train them to be communicators.

Voices from the Trenches

"Key to my youth group experience was the varied number of opportunities for us students to grow with one another, as well as to serve outside the church. The majority of our time was spent either in the Word led by caring, invested, volunteer adults from our church body in our S.L.U.G (Senior Leaders Under God) group or serving in the community through mission trips, also led by adult volunteers in our church. The impact of the time spent in these opportunities is something that I will carry with me for the rest of my life and that I desperately hope and intend for my kids to have."

—Ainslie, church volunteer, lawyer,
and former youth group member

Ways to Train

BJ likes to have a once-a-month gathering of his volunteers. Anne has trouble getting her team together, so they meet fifteen minutes before youth group and fifteen minutes after the event.

Marvin has a team approach in which no individual can be on several teams. So he has a set-up team, prayer team, administrative team, teaching team, and small-group team. He has a once-a-month meeting with his volunteers, and each team meets with him for about thirty minutes (it's an all-morning task Saturday for Marvin but only thirty minutes on Saturday for those on each team with selected time slots).

Archie communicates his vision to his team through weekly e-mails and texts and requires a yearly one-day equipping and training retreat for volunteers.

The bottom line for training is this: there is not a one-size-fits-all model. I have tried many different methods and have found that what worked in Ohio didn't work in Oklahoma and that some things that worked in Kentucky did work in South Carolina.

Find what works best for you and your team.

How to Honor, Keep, Affirm, and Fire

Volunteers are not paid, therefore they have limited time and access. Part of the joy of being a volunteer is having the freedom to say, "I won't be here the next three weeks. I am snorkeling in Hawaii."

So the paid youth worker, once he's worked through his resentment, must find ways to appreciate and honor volunteers. Here are a few ways that have been helpful to me (I have been paid and also have served as a volunteer):

1. People want to be thanked not so much publicly but privately. So let them know how much you appreciate them.

2. Send them texts or voice mails with a "thanks so much" message and personalize it.

3. Once a year send all your volunteers a small gift card. An organization I serve sends me a Starbucks card once a year and it's not at Christmas. I really like that!

4. Serve volunteers with a thank-you banquet at which the students are the servers.

5. Make sure in your job descriptions that each volunteer gets a few weeks off per year (some ministries give most of the summer off if there are paid interns).

6. Send your volunteers to training events to encourage and equip them. One time my church in Oklahoma paid for forty

adult volunteers to attend a one-day Youth Specialties conference. By the end of the day, my adults were stoked for another year of youth ministry!

7. Letting a volunteer go is an unpleasant experience most of the time, but it can be redeeming. I had to "fire" a volunteer once because of some inappropriate hugging and poor boundaries with teenagers. Most of the time firing should be a *last resort*. Moral and ethical issues usually warrant a time away and then possibly a reentry time if the person is genuinely repentant.

Voices from the Trenches

"Teenagers already don't trust adults. Youth ministry doesn't need more chaperones to make sure everyone behaves or nothing gets broken. Youth ministry needs adults who love teenagers and are willing to step into teenage culture. Teenage culture is messy and full of things that will make us uncomfortable and break our hearts, but we must be willing to go. Jesus came into this world to take lives that are broken, messed up, and empty and to redeem them. Youth ministry can no longer expect teens to be drawn to church; we must be willing to enter their world with the love of Christ."

—Brent, paid youth worker

Have Job Descriptions

When I discovered that volunteers needed job descriptions, some of my people balked. "Why should I have a job description? You're not paying me." True, but a job description is more about what they *aren't* expected to do than anything else.

We can either *develop* or *destroy* volunteers. Explaining a volunteer's time commitment and expectations is one way to develop a volunteer; and when there is no job explanation, it can kill the ministry and destroy the volunteer's loyalty and integrity (see sample job descriptions at the end of the chapter). Some individuals don't commit for this simple reason: there are no clear guidelines on when the "job begins and ends." If someone thinks the job is "eternal" (with no ending in sight), he or she may well choose golf over ministry—and who could blame him or her?

Learn to Delegate Well

A great leader trusts his or her teammates and learns to delegate appropriately. We see Nehemiah delegating responsibilities to hundreds of people as they rebuilt the broken walls of Jerusalem (see Nehemiah 4–5).

Learn to delegate well and utilize people, but don't use them. I know some folk who have felt manipulated and walked on as a volunteer.

Find areas in which you need help and delegate those responsibilities. For example, I am pretty inept in the area of technology. To this day I have never learned *purposefully* to create slides for talks, seminars, and sermons. I am sure I could learn and maybe even become proficient at it, but I *don't want to learn*, because if I did learn how to do it, then I'd spend hours creating cool, masterful graphics for talks instead of preparing for the messages. So I have intentionally been "dumb and dumber" in the area of graphic design. I have found several people who simply love doing this kind of art behind the scenes and they feel it is a ministry to me, so I have gladly accepted their gift to me!

It's not like graphic design is beneath me or that going to pick up basketballs at Walmart at midnight is not productive; it's just that some things need to be delegated—for your sake and for the sake of your volunteers.

Voices from the Trenches

"Many of our youth are coming from non-Christian and broken homes. To meet some of the relationship and family needs of our youth, we must be open to and pursue volunteers of all ages and stages. On a mission trip to South Africa, I observed a woman from my church in her fifties ministering to youth. Always being on the lookout for quality youth leaders, I asked her if she had ever considered volunteering with our senior high ministry. She looked stunned and said, 'But I'm a grandma?!' I told her, 'The youth would love you! Why don't you come to our fall retreat and give it a try?' She came and started leading our girls for several years. She told me that it never occurred to her that God could use her to minister to teens. If we are open to God's leading, you and others may be surprised whom God has called to serve."

—Karen, professor of youth ministry, family, and culture

Q's to Encourage

1. What are some of the mistakes you've made in recruiting adult volunteers?

2. What is the best way you have found to recruit volunteers?

3. What practical things can you do to affirm and keep your volunteers?

Sample Job Description

1. Sound Engineer

    a. Be a growing Christian and involved in the life of the church.

    b. Attend the twice-a-year training sessions for youth ministry volunteers.

    c. Complete the application form and background check.

2. Job Responsibilities

    a. Attend the weekly youth meeting to run the sound system and graphic designs.

    b. Be at least one hour early each Sunday to make sure all the equipment is turned off before you leave.

    c. Train an apprentice to help assist and be present when you cannot attend.

    d. You will be given the month of June for summertime play and family time.

    e. The time commitment is for one year (September–May or July and August.) At that time you will meet with the youth leader in charge to assess if you want to continue in this position.

We appreciate your interest in this position.
Thanks,
The Youth Ministry Team

Youth Ministry Volunteer Application Form

Name _____

Address _____

City _____ State _____

Zip code _____

Primary phone _____

Alternate phone:_____

Education: Describe briefly your education background.

What year did you graduate from high school?

College degree?

Graduate or Seminary Degree?

Feel free to use separate sheets for any of your answers.

1. Give a brief summary of your Christian journey.

2. What are some of the strengths and skill sets you bring if you were to work in student ministry?

3. Where will you thrive in student ministry?

4. What areas of youth ministry will be a struggle for you?

5. List the last three jobs you've held and a reference of one person from each workplace who knows your character and work ethic.

6. List any recent ministry or leadership experiences in the church.

7. Where have you been challenged and stretched in your life in the past year?

8. In your own words, explain what it means to be a follower of Jesus.

9. Describe some of the qualities you have that make you a great candidate to work with students and families.

10. What is the most recent book you have read that inspired you or made you think?

11. What do you like and dislike about teenagers?

12. What are some ways you can impact a teenager in our ministry?

13. Have you ever had any drug charges, felonies, or arrests? If yes, please explain.

Please list three personal references and their contact information:

_____

_____

_____

Chapter Seven

STUDENTS LIKE KATIE
BEYOND INGROWN CHRISTIANITY

"We are happy with the size of our group. We'll take one or two more, but that's it."
—a male student from a high school ministry of eight students

"We'll take one or two more, but that's it." These words blew me away. It was actually said by a junior in high school from a church that called me in for consulting. I was shocked, aghast, and appalled. I could not believe what I had just heard.

This medium-size church had the classic "ingrown toenail," a stay-within-the-four-walls-of-the-church syndrome. The youth group kids were "afraid of getting too big." They had less than fifteen students on a good day.

I have a feeling it may have looked like one of the religious groups of Jesus' day—the Pharisees. One of those exclusive, hard-to-break-into kinds of groups. Perhaps a bit too smug, somewhat judgmental, and one that certainly needed to work on inclusiveness.

What's the Problem?

When youth groups feel superior or better than other groups, they have become ingrown. A youth group that doesn't want to grow or change and that resists letting new people in is what I call a "holy huddle." When we speak in sociological terms, we think of phrases such as *egocentric*, which indicate that the group is all about themselves.

Groups that become *ethnocentric* have become combative and resistant to outsiders and people who look, act, or think differently.

All too many Christian youth groups have become cliquish and cluster focused rather than taking an outside-focused approach. We have become isolated when it comes to serving, evangelism, outreach, and missions.

Problem #7 of American Youth Ministry:
We've created a "holy huddle."

Maybe it should be called the "unholy" huddle because if a group does not want outsiders to become insiders and the youth do not want to do anything outside of the four walls of the church building, that has some kind of impact that reeks of *non-holiness*.

Jesus was the most *holy* person who ever walked on the planet, and he involved himself with the poor, disenfranchised, prostitutes, and tax collectors (one of the most despised groups in his day). He was known as "a friend of tax collectors and sinners" (Luke 7:34).

The common people *liked* Jesus. He was invited to parties with the outcasts and to drink wine at wedding festivals (and supplied extra wine that night!) Jesus hung out with the unlikeable and unpopular. He was accused of being a winebibber and a blasphemer, and he continually found himself in places that traditional rabbis avoided.

It gives a new definition to *holiness*, doesn't it? Here's my definition of *holiness*: "To be holy is to stay connected to God while we connect with people who are disinterested in God."

Finding a Solution

Youth ministry is not about creating a youth group but instead creating a movement. Groups that are only interested in focusing inwardly will die a slow death. God's intent has always been about growth and change. True discipleship goes from the inner world to the outer world. True disciples of Jesus care about others.

Youth ministries have the potential to do great evangelism in their local schools, but they should also affect their state, region, and ultimately the rest of the United States.

The American church has resources to change the world. Our problem is inward. But the solution is outward. Youth ministry is intended to become a movement, not a monument.

Solution to Employ:

Youth ministry needs to go beyond the four walls.

Create Awareness: Go Glo-cal

The term *glo-cal* has the idea of incorporating the value of serving people both globally and locally. Mission trips and service projects are designed to create awareness and exposure. Youth ministries can make a difference by identifying local and global needs. Always begin with your community. What needs are present that don't seem to go away or that others neglect? Consider such issues as homelessness, AIDS, refugees, and the poor. Think about issues of justice and acts of kindness and proceed to go local and global. Go glo-cal.

Understanding the Global Economy

At the ripe age of fifteen years old, Katie took an active leadership role in our youth ministry. Katie had a heart for the poor and would gladly give away her possessions to anyone in need. One day she came to our youth staff wanting to make a difference. Instead of assigning an adult to oversee and drive the project, we told Katie that we believed she could handle the challenge.

She took charge.

Acts of service and kindness help students understand the world we live in. When American students realize how much they have and what the rest of the world doesn't have, they become more compassionate.

Called to Be Generous

Our sinful nature is to be greedy. But our new nature is to be giving. Jesus modeled for us a life of generosity. One cannot be fully fulfilled when he or she is totally selfish: "You are familiar with the generosity of our Master, Jesus Christ. Rich as he was, he gave it all away for us—in one stroke he became poor and we became rich" (2 Corinthians 8:9, *The Message*).

Make a Difference

Deep within themselves youth want to make a difference. They won't care about things they don't know about, so it's imperative that the leaders of "big church" and youth group make students aware of the needs in the world.

World Vision started the "Let It Growl" thirty-hour fasting program for world hunger in order to help students experience hunger on a personal level. Students gather together collectively to fast and then take the monies and food they would have used for "food consumption" and give it to the ministry of World Vision.

Voices from the Trenches

"Break out of the holy huddle by using your best offense: your students! Each Friday night after home football games, hundreds of students attend an after-party event that our youth ministry hosts. Our biggest outreach move of the year was having students from our ministry attend this event specifically to welcome their peers and invite them to one of our programming nights. By using students already in your care, you multiply your outreach abilities and show students that they are valuable in expanding the kingdom!"

—Kristina, paid youth worker

Expose Cultural Encapsulation

It's easy to get culturally encapsulated, so do what you can to fight it. We are spoiled Americans. During one of my first trips to Haiti and the Dominican Republic, our students were involved with constructing a church building. We worked hard daily, and some Haitians and Dominicans helped for free while others watched us.

What our students didn't realize is that these underemployed Dominicans and Haitians would have gladly done the work for *pay*, yet in reality we were stealing their chance to make money to support their families. We prided ourselves, but I could sense in some of their faces a sense of humiliation. I wondered if they were thinking, *Americans are taking our dignity away, and they think we cannot help ourselves.*

Cultural encapsulation is a way of thinking and perceiving. It goes something like this:

- "I have all the latest in computer and technological gadgets; everyone in the world must have them."

- "Our family vacations in exotic places, therefore the rest of the world takes vacations."

In *Who Lives in the Global Village?* Donella Meadows says that if the world's population were boiled down to 100 people, these are the numbers we'd be dealing with:

- Out of 100 people, the village consists of 60 Asians, 14 Africans, 12 Europeans, 8 Latin Americans, 5 from America and Canada, and 1 from the South Pacific.

- 67 are illiterate, 50 are malnourished, and 1 is dying of starvation.

- 33 have no access to safe water supplies.

- 24 don't have any electricity.

- 7 have access to the Internet.

- 1 has a college education.

- 1 has HIV[1]

Rethink Wealth

Unfortunately Americans seem to misunderstand how the "rest" of the world lives. Check out www.globalrichlist.com. A teacher in America making $50,000 is among the top 1 percent of the richest people in the world! A high school student in America making minimum wage at twenty hours a week is making more money than 85 percent of the people in the global world.

My eyes, ears, and heart had a difficult reentry into America after taking my first trip to Haiti. Going to the poorest country in the Western Hemisphere was radical enough for our youth group and me. But the most unsettling time was arriving back in the Miami airport, seeing all the food options and Americans griping and complaining about late flights, poor service on planes, and business deals gone bad. We are the richest nation on earth, and I had just spent a week living on the floor of the home of a pastor who makes $300 dollars a year!

Overseas Mission: More Than a Vacation

Short-term missions in youth ministry have gone pretty well when the goal is for exposure and creating a long-term, lifetime relationship with that particular people group. But short-term missions become a waste of time and energy when they are viewed as vacations. I have also been to Mexico, Spain, Venezuela, Belize, Europe, Barbados, and ten other countries. It never ceases to amaze me how easily a "mission trip" can start looking like a holiday trip or an entertaining escape.

One of the first overseas mission trips I experienced with a youth group was a mixture of mission, service projects, some evangelism, and construction projects. One of the main discussions from both students and adults was concerning how to end the trip. It turned out for the past fifteen years, the final day of the trip was a play day at the beach. I have no problem with playing on a mission trip, but when all the students could talk about was the beach experience, and the majority of the video footage (shown during all church services) shows teens playing sand volleyball and hanging out in the ocean instead of serving the poor, then I have an upset stomach!

Missions are not about a short-term vacation. They are about being an ambassador of Jesus Christ to the lost.

Voices from the Trenches

"I would ask, 'What is the rest of the church already doing locally and globally?' Years ago when I arrived at a church as a youth pastor, I asked lots of questions to discover and learn what had already been happening in the youth ministry prior to my arrival (always a good thing to do). One of the things I discovered was that the youth ministry's local and global outreach was completely separate from the larger church's outreach ministry. The youth had separate service projects, separate short-term mission trips to separate countries, and on it went. Our church had more than ten missionaries serving all over the world, but the youth ministry was not going (or offering) to go support our missionaries.

"I quickly changed this by asking the person overseeing our missionaries how we could help her. Youth ministry should not disconnect and reinvent the wheel of outreach. It should connect with the whole church. There is a powerful opportunity when teens and adults serve together and share the gospel close and far, not to mention a unified purpose for the whole church."

—Jeff, pastor of local outreach

Leadership Discernment

Be wise stewards of your resources. One of the obvious juxtapositions is the tension of local versus overseas needs. Finance committees will ask the valid question: "Why are we spending $15,000 on going to Guatemala when we have the poor and unreached in our own community within five miles of us?"

Good point.

These are very delicate questions. And my response is fairly simple: each faith community must lean on the leaders to find their "sweet spot" and calling. The leadership team of the church must discern where to invest globally and locally.

I know of some churches who pour 80 percent of their resources locally and others who pour 80 percent outside of the United States. One church I partner with invests much of their budget into Costa Rica. Whether the mission's focus is local, Haiti, Eastern Europe, or West Africa, it is vitally important that the leadership determines where God is leading that particular body of Christians.

Voices from the Trenches

"One of our goals is to get kids experiencing serving beyond the four walls. We do this both locally and globally.

"Locally: At the end of each school year, our youth organize a food drive for the local mobile food pantry that delivers food to needy children during the summer months. We provide a recommended shopping list of food items to the congregation of healthy, easy-to-prepare items to donate.

"Globally: The students selected a child to sponsor through Compassion International. They now have a name and face of a little girl in Indonesia with whom to exchange letters and for whom to pray, as well as have the opportunity to learn about another part of the world. Every Sunday we collect money and pray for 'Tati.'"

—Karen, professor of youth ministry, family, and culture

Peer Evangelism

Over the decades, youth leaders have been frustrated because their students don't share their faith easily or at all. We have seen the statistics that most American Christians don't share Christ often.

I don't think *guilt* works well as a motivator for evangelism.

I don't believe *threatening* people with hell works either.

I do know *ownership* works. When an individual owns something, you cannot take it away. I have seen students who have a thirst and desire to know God and make Jesus known, but sometimes zeal and passion aren't enough. What cements the desire for peer evangelism is when knowledge and application meet head-on.

It's called training.

Train Them

Teens who encounter Jesus will want to be a witness to others, but there are good chances the student is emotionally and spiritually immature and will need some practical training on evangelism. Those who are more relational and extraverted will want to make it happen. When teens catch a vision for sharing their faith, please train them, then get out of their way and let them drive it!

The organization Dare to Share seeks to empower teens to naturally share their faith. There are all kinds of resources to help students know the basics of the faith and how to give it away. Allow your students to make mistakes; give them the freedom to succeed and fail. Evangelism is about sharing the story of God, which also includes our story.

When young people get excited about the good news of the gospel and have experienced the forgiveness of sins and their lives being changed (usually with baby steps), they will want to tell somebody.

Be patient with the process and don't pressure them to evangelize. If you have good news, you cannot help but share it. If you love someone, you will eventually tell others about that "one." And once you start telling your story, it influences the person listening to live it.

Ownership comes through training, experience, and awareness. Not only will keeping them in the youth room not impact them for eternity, but getting them to share their faith will.

Voices from the Trenches

"When students get the opportunity to serve, whatever their capacity is, it challenges them in a way like nothing else I have ever seen. It is no longer just about what they have heard or been told. Giving students chances to invest somewhere helps them discover that they have purpose in life. They have an opportunity to connect to something bigger—an opportunity to see that God has called them to be more than just a part of the church, but to *be* the church.

"The question now becomes 'How can we as student pastors and volunteers create more of these opportunities?' We must alter our schedules, budgets, and priorities to allow for more serving opportunities. If we truly believe that putting a student in the environment of serving is life changing, then it must become one of the most important things in our ministries.

We can no longer ignore the fact that students still walk away from their faith. This means that we need to create a new culture in student ministry: a culture of serving. We must become known for what we do, not what we say."

—Brent, paid youth worker

Get Offensive

Have your youth ministry pick a human horror and go on the offensive. Kids in our youth ministry support Compassion International by adopting several children. A group down the street is concerned about human trafficking.

Every day children all over the globe walk miles for clean water.
Every day kids all over the planet look for a meal.
Every day young kids are being sexually abused.

What jacks you up? Ignites fire in your belly? What injustice keeps you awake at night? Get your students involved, and I guarantee that some of them will take up the mantle of servanthood and justice for the sake of the gospel.

Voices from the Trenches

"Students today are constantly bombarded with information. They are being reminded of social issues through media and the Internet. As Christians we have the greatest opportunity and responsibility to get students passionate about the cause of Jesus. We can organize mission trips and outreach events as a practical response for students to get involved in the greatest cause. They know people in their schools, on their sports teams, and on summer mission trips who need to hear the gospel. Usually, the issue isn't about them knowing the need; it is more about them doing something about it. Let's not bombard them with information; let's give them practical opportunities to be missional while reaching out to others!"

—Grace Marie, paid youth worker

Set the Bar High for Students

- There are some incredible stories of world changers from those who are under fourteen years of age. For instance:

- Ten-year-old Talia Leman started a fundraising campaign of ten million to help victims of Hurricane Katrina.[2]

- Jordan Foxworthy, age fourteen, started the Bite Back Campaign to encourage her peers to give $10 to buy mosquito nets to save people from malaria.[3]

- Austin Gutwein established Hoops of Hope and raised money to build health clinics in Africa. Austin is fourteen years old.[4]

- Zack Hunter began Loose Change to Loosen Chains at age twelve to stop human trafficking.[5]

- Jamie Coleman started Walk Humbly to send shoes to Kenya, and four thousand pairs of shoes were sent. Did I mention that Jamie was a teenager?[6]

Earlier in this chapter I mentioned Katie, a girl who had a vision for Africa and for clean water to drink. Over a period of a few months, we forgot about Katie's passion, and then we learned "through the youth group grapevine" that Katie and several other girls and guys from our youth ministry had raised close to $20,000 to dig four wells in Africa to distribute clean water. Katie and her friends single-handedly helped save lives. Katie went on to Wheaton College to major in poverty studies and plans on being a medical doctor overseas.

Let's break out of the "holy huddle" and make an eternal impact. Youth ministry is going beyond the four walls! Let's get it right.

Voices from the Trenches

"If we are going to be honest, the majority of Christian American teenagers have one thing in mind about their faith: themselves. If a leader stresses the point that his or her faith isn't just about improving themselves, then more kids will be willing to go out and share their faith. Many Christians in general have lost their urgency for evangelism. It is something God calls for everyone, not just for the select extroverted 'super Christians.' Once American youth groups learn that it is not all about them and that God calls everyone to evangelize, they will break free from the four walls."

—Wesley, high school student

Q's to Employ

1. What local needs exist in your community that your youth ministry can help with?

2. What global issues does your congregation have a heart for?

3. What specific steps do you need to take to be in mission locally and globally?

Notes

1. From *Technical Report*, Hartland, Vermont, Sustainability Institute, 2005, mentioned in David Livermore and Terry Linhart, *What Can We Do?*

Practical Ways Your Youth Ministry Can Have a Global Conscience (Grand Rapids, MI: Zondervan, 2011).

2. David Livermore and Terry Linhart, *What Can We Do? Practical Ways Your Youth Ministry Can Have a Global Conscience* (Grand Rapids, MI: Zondervan, 2011), 148-49.

3. Ibid.
4. Ibid.
5. Ibid.
6. Ibid.

Chapter Eight

FIRST OPINIONS AND MALACHI THE ITALIAN PROPHET

My people are destroyed from lack of knowledge.
Because you have rejected knowledge, I also reject you as my priests
because you have ignored the law of your God, I also will ignore your children.
—Hosea 4:6

The youth pastor told his kids to turn to the First Book of Opinions. Nobody laughed; no one flinched. Some looked. Some went to the table of contents. One kid shouted, "I don't think it's in the Bible." The majority did not know. Some still searched for the missing book. It was not in the Bible, but the group didn't get it. We are biblically illiterate in our country and in our churches. It's safe to say that most Americans do not know the Bible very well, nor do those who attend churches. The Bible is getting dusty, and our students don't seem to care. What's gone wrong with our culture when it comes to reading and understanding the Bible?

What's the Problem?

Whether an American teenager attends Sunday school, youth group, Young Life, Youth for Christ, Fellowship of Christian Athletes, or Wednesday night youth group, adolescents do not know their Bibles.

The average youth group leader probably gives one to two biblical messages a week, but the retention rate is fairly low. The talking-head model is having limited impact. We talk, and students listen. And it might be great for our egos to entertain them and make them laugh, but do they take anything home with them?

We're a spiritually undiscerning and seemingly unconcerned youth culture when it comes to reading and understanding and applying God's book.

We seem allergic to the Bible, or are we scared of it? Some are intimidated by the "bigness" of the Scriptures and others are too apathetic to care.

Parents of teens and their parents are not in any better shape.

Problem #8 of American Youth Ministry:
Biblically illiterate Christians.

Finding a Solution

Jesus battled the devil in the wilderness, and his source of victory was the word of God. Three times Satan threw a temptation at the Messiah, and three times Jesus quoted the Bible (the book of Deuteronomy, actually) back at the enemy with "It is written" (Matthew 4:1-10).

The church has always believed that God's book is authoritative. Historically every church service has been filled with the reading of the Scriptures. We read and teach and train students in order for the listeners to be transformed, not just informed: "For the word of God is living and active. Sharper than any double-edged sword, it penetrates even to dividing soul and spirit, joints and marrow; it judges the thoughts and attitudes of the heart" (Hebrews 4:12).

Solution to Experience:
Use creative Bible teaching and training, not just entertainment.

What do we want to produce in youth? Ultimately we are aiming at building self-sustaining disciples of Jesus. We want these students to ideally love Jesus, share their faith, and reproduce their faith into others into their adult years. We want students to mature in such a way that if they ever get married and become parents, they will disciple their children, and onto their next generation. That is our prayer and dream. Our vision is not only the years of adolescence; we are shooting for something much deeper and wider: life-long learning and training in the word of God.

Here are ten ways to get it right on creative teaching and training, not just entertainment.

1. Host a Once-a-Month Youth-Led Night

This is a simple event that has huge dividends. I stumbled on it in my first youth ministry. I was getting overwhelmed with teaching three times a week, and my volunteers looked tired, so I asked some of my core students if they would lead a Sunday night meeting. They reluctantly agreed.

What started as an innocent "let's try something new and different" became a staple event on the last Sunday of the month. We called it "Youth-Led Night" (flashy, huh?).

The students would lead games, lead worship, and share their stories, and someone would preach. It was amazing in the sense that it was imperfect. Kids would forget the words of the song, our emcee farted publicly on stage once, and one speaker couldn't find his notes. These nights had the highest attendance of all the meetings we organized.

I remember Jan (a senior in high school) telling me how scared she was to speak in front of youth group on a youth-led night. So we helped her with the planning and how to analyze the biblical text, find the big idea in it, and come up with a story or two that would minister to her peers. Little did I know that she invited her entire senior class to come support her at church for that evening. Over fifty of her classmates came to hear Jan teach at youth group.

That night I drank the Kool-aid.

Youth in ministry to youth. Peer to peer, student to student. Maybe that's really why it's called youth ministry. Students doing the ministry.

2. Have a Student Read the Bible Out Loud Instead of You

I never read the Bible passage before I speak anymore. I let students do it. This might sound silly and ridiculous, but instead of the paid person reading or an adult volunteer reading the Bible out loud, why not have a student read it? I have done this hundreds, if not thousands, of times before a message or Bible study. It is remarkable for a few reasons.

Some students never read the Bible. If a kid has shown up to one of your youth meetings, ask him or her beforehand if he or she would read a passage of Scripture before you speak. I think I have been turned down maybe once in my lifetime.

What has been fun is to see a middle school boy get up and read a verse and maybe even stumble through it. When he is done reading out loud, without any prodding or pushing, the crowd starts clapping for the student who just read. I mean, I have never received a clap "offering" by reading the Bible, but students will applaud their friends.

I am not saying we let kids read up-front in order to get applause, but it suggests to me that the audience was trying to honor the Bible and the reader. And what happens to the reader? Nobody probably knows, except I have a feeling that the student is getting God's word inside him or her a little more than if he or she had just sat in the audience and listened to me read it.

It gets them into the Word a little bit more than normal. For the teen-ager, speaking God's word has the power of creating interest that might lead them to read the Bible when they get home.

3. Embrace the Power of Student Leadership

One of the most impressive scenes I have witnessed is when I ask high school guys to start a Bible study for middle school boys. I determined years ago that when a high school student leads anything, middle school students listen and take note.

In order to be in my senior-guys-only group called SLUG (Senior Leaders under God), each senior is given a list of five to ten middle school students on the church youth group list. For weeks I teach and train them how to lead a small group, especially for middle school boys.

It is a struggle for these guys to make the phone call (or text) to the boys and then pull together a group of junior high guys and figure out when to meet, what time, where, and then how to engage each of them. What a challenge, but most of my guys pulled it off.

If the church wants to see guys lead, then we need to let them do it. Remember the axiom: things are more caught than taught.

Jason was in my SLUG group, and he poured into a handful of boys. Fast-forward several years, and today, here is what the members of that small junior high group are up to today: Sam is serving overseas as a mis-sionary; Micah is a teacher and basketball coach; Josh is serving as a chap-lain in the Army; Jared is an attorney and leader in the church; Trey is a church planter; and James is a youth pastor. All from one small group of junior high boys serving Jesus!

Voices from the Trenches

"We need to be gospel focused in all we do. The gospel of Jesus not only saves us from sin at a youth retreat but also sustains and informs the whole church where to go and what to do, including youth ministry. This requires us to fall in love again with our first love, Jesus. This will increase our passion for Him and thus the word of God. With this first love, we begin to teach and live the gospel in front of the youth and parents in our ministry. This has to be the starting point for helping teens become more biblically literate. With renewed passion, we need to teach the 'whole story' of the Bible, not just verses. Many of the younger generations need to be taught or relearn how the divine tapestry of God is woven together. This can be done by teaching the Bible in sections for the purpose of teens seeing the glory of God and how they fit into this plan for the world."

—Jeff, pastor of local outreach

4. Challenge Kids to Small-Group Bible Memorization

One lost art today is Scripture memory. Start a small group with the purpose of learning and memorizing parts of the Bible. It could be one passage from a book of the Bible. As a young follower of Jesus, I started memorizing one verse from Matthew 1 (a passage that I would choose). Then I memorized one verse from Matthew 2 and then one verse from chapter 3. It took me two years to memorize one verse from every chapter in the New Testament all the way through Revelation.

This is not that impressive, for I know some people who have memorized entire books of the Bible. The point isn't how much information one retains. What is essential is that we get people feeding on God's word. As we get into the Word, the Word gets into us. As one friend of mine says, "We read the Bible not to finish, but to change."

5. Challenge Your Students with the Message of "4 for 1"

For students to experience the Word, I challenge them to read Mark 2. I want students to start early in life the visionary process of dreaming for others to encounter Jesus.

Mark 2 includes the fascinating story of four men who have a vision for one man to hear the word of God. Large numbers gathered to hear Jesus teach, but there was a problem: the room was packed (if we only had this problem!). Using some creative evangelism, the four men lowered the one man who was paralyzed on a stretcher through the roof.

In Jesus' day, rooms were easy to break into, and so these men became roof breakers and roof removers. Jesus was "in the house," and all of a sudden a man is being lowered from the top of the building into the room where Jesus, *the word of God,* was teaching.

What was Jesus' reaction? "When Jesus saw their faith, he said to the paralyzed man, 'Son, your sins are forgiven'" (Mark 2:5). We do not know who the four men are, nor do we know the relationship they have with the sick man. We also know nothing about the paralyzed man other than he cannot walk.

He cannot get to Jesus, that is, unless someone else gets him to the Messiah. Enter four men who take a risk, who don't play it safe, and who end up wrecking some nice old Jewish lady's ceiling. They break the roof and remove it.

A youth ministry ceases to be an effective ministry when the word of God is not taught and communicated. A youth ministry will fail to bear fruit if our students don't get into the Word and let the Word get into them. I am not talking about raising up a generation of religious Bible thumpers or Pharisees who know Leviticus Bible trivia.

I want my students to so love God's word that they want to find the "paralyzed" students in their schools—those kids who don't fit in or who sit all alone in the cafeteria—to be sought out and brought to Jesus.

The Bible does not tell us much of the four men. All we know is they had one goal: get the paralyzed man to the feet of Jesus and then this man will get healed!

What engages me about this story is that these four men had a vision. All it took was a dream for one person to have an encounter with Jesus. A radical healing occurs, not just of his body, but of his soul. His sins are forgiven, not because of anything he has done, but because of the faith of the four men.

Youth ministry is about challenging students to the "4 to 1" principle—that is, going after one spiritually paralyzed individual and removing whatever roofs it takes to get that person to Jesus.

"It saddens me to see so many students graduating from youth programs but still not understanding how to study their Bibles. A few years ago I began to realize how many students didn't understand the narrative of the Bible. My ministry partner and I decided to dedicate a full school year of teaching through the overall story at our program night. So many of them knew lots of Bible stories but didn't understand how and where they all fit together. We made it creative with videos and visuals to keep them intrigued, and each lesson built on the previous one. Some would say it was risky to do this because students aren't typically interested in an overview of the Bible. So many students ended up loving it and learning something that I believe it will stick with them. This kind of teaching curriculum takes serious planning and intentionality, and the end result is worth it."

—Grace Marie, paid youth worker

6. Understand Learning Styles

As an educator, I think that we have a biblical illiteracy problem that is related to our lack of acknowledging and using different learning styles. Now I understand that entire books have been written on this subject, so I would like to keep this simple by identifying the styles I have observed primarily with students ages ten to twenty years old. Consider these four dominant learning styles: auditory, discussion oriented, visual, and experiential.

Auditory learners gain insight by listening and taking it in through note taking and processing. Think of the word *ears* when you hear the word auditory. Auditory students learn by hearing and taking notes and applying the information. When teaching is primarily speaking (verbal) to listening ears, students forget what they hear within a day or two. Sometimes I cannot remember a sermon I have heard a day later (sometimes I cannot remember my own!).

Discussion-oriented learners are guided by the *mouth*; they need to talk about and debrief their experiences, and they learn by dialogue and hearing others' ideas. These teens want deep discussion and are engaged in talking with peers and adults.

The third kind of learning style is *visual*, so think about what is seen.

Our culture has increasingly become more visual with technology. If I am speaking at youth group or church and show a movie clip, the visual learners who were checked out all of a sudden are back in!

The fourth style of learning is the *experiential learner*. If auditory learners are guided by their ears and discussion-oriented learners are engaged by their mouths and visual learners are dialed in by their eyes, then the experiential learner uses his or her *feet*. Experiential students, who are by nature dynamic learners, discover by *doing*, that is, going on mission trips, teaching a class, or leading a game. A lecture will bore them, and a small group might intimidate them. Experiential learners need something to do.

The problem we have is that people teach like they learn. If youth worker Diana is an auditory learner, her predisposition will be to lecture. If Kyle is a discussion learner, he will employ small groups every second he can. Marvin is an experiential learner and will use ropes courses, games, and initiatives for fifty-two weeks out of the year. And Courtney, being a visual learner, is looking for clips from *Remember the Titans* or from *Spiderman* to show at a small group.

Not only do we teach like we learn, but also we tend to ignore the other styles of learning. So you might be wondering, how does this relate to biblical illiteracy?

Why do I bring learning styles up? I am convinced that we end up missing how our students learn, so biblical "intelligence" is on the down low. We need to mix things up. Let's say your youth ministry has 75 percent experiential learners, yet the dominant way of teaching is lecture and a little discussion. Can you guess what the retention will be? Maybe close to zero.

Biblical retention and application might be the simple result of being flexible on understanding learning styles. Try this for a month:

- Week One: Make youth group 80 percent experiential by serving at a soup kitchen.

- Week Two: Use discussion as a primary mode of teaching and utilize some small groups.

- Week Three: Use a lecture, video clip, and application.

- Week Four: Your group watches part of an engaging movie and you process it.

- Week Five: Put your hand to all four learning styles and expect some mass chaos! Have fun and knock it out of the park.

My point is: involve *as many* different learning styles *and mix it up with variety* so we can up the ante on Biblical literacy.

7. High School Students Learn Best by Teaching and Mentoring Younger Students

Allison was a freshman in high school and one day expressed how much she "hated Sunday school." Of course, I understood most of us youth workers tend to dislike it as well. I inquired why, and she said the "teacher was boring and didn't know anything."

I asked Allison if she thought she could do better, to which she replied, "Yes, absolutely." So I put Allison to the test. One of our husband-wife friends was teaching the fifth-grade Sunday school class, so I asked if Allison could sit in and shadow them and perhaps get a chance to teach. It turned out that for the next four years of high school, Allison would never step inside the high school Sunday school again because she was transformed by teaching fifth-graders.

We learn best by teaching. The teacher always "learns" more than the listener.

There is something about teaching a younger and moldable student, like a piece of clay shaped by the potter.

Teens often learn best by experience and doing, so why not involve them in working with younger kids? My experience with short-term mission trips is that when we debrief the trip, the number-one "most talked about event" was directly proportional to working with younger kids.

I have heard this kind of line now for over thirty years of ministry by a teenager: "My time using drama and Bible stories in the vacation Bible outreach was life changing. Those little kids grabbed my heart."

Voices from the Trenches

"In order to produce students in your ministry who really understand the Bible, you have to be intentional. You don't just fall into training students in biblical literacy. Start with a strategy for training. What are the important elements to have involved in this training? Will it be through small groups, program nights, or one-on-one discipleship? After you have a strategy, create a system. What books do you cover first? How long is the training time? Can your plan be sustained by the teachers involved?

Voices from the Trenches, Cont.

"One of the best strategies I have seen implemented is a chapter-by-chapter approach during which students are at tables with adult leaders. There is a master teacher who walks the group through a chapter of a book. At intervals throughout the chapter, the students will have the opportunity to discuss questions with their leader, look up commentary on verses, and research words present through a Bible dictionary. Through this approach students are learning not only what the Bible says but also how to study it for themselves."

—Trevor, paid youth worker

---

8. Have Student "Interns"

Lindsey and Marty were my first high school interns. They were basically glorified volunteers with a small stipend ($50 per week). I figured if McDonald's and Wendy's could provide training to high school juniors and seniors, so could our church.

We put these juniors and seniors into situations of serving the church but also of teaching the Bible. That's right: we paid students to do their own Bible study and teach others. It was great! They learned the Word and actually got paid for it. I mean, don't we do that today with pastors and professors and teachers?

Voices from the Trenches

"What would happen if youth ministry modeled to the rest of the world creative Bible teaching that is fun, engaging, interactive, and relevant? What if every Bible lesson and sermon had a chance to discuss ways to implement and apply the truth just delivered? What would it look like if everyone had a chance to talk about what they are learning and how they are struggling and growing? Students and adults actually might want to come to church."

—Sam, professor of youth ministry, family, and culture

---

9. Parents Discuss Their Faith Story

Kara Powell and Chap Clark clarify in their exceptional book *Sticky Faith: Everyday Ideas to Build Lasting Faith in Your Kids* that "students whose parents talk about faith have more sticky faith."[1]

The epidemic we have discovered is that most teens and their parents rarely discuss faith issues.

The Search Institute interviewed eleven thousand teenagers and found that "12 percent of youth have a regular dialogue with their mom on faith or life issues." That's about one out of eight teens who talks with his or her mom about the life of faith. It is less with fathers: one out of twenty kids talks with his or her dad about the faith, around 5 percent.[2]

Powell and Clark learned that parents tend to avoid touchy subjects and are afraid to share their faith journey and doubts. Powell and Clark suggest that a kid's faith will stick better if a parent would consider the following ideas:

- Talk about doubts.

- Learn to listen and ask questions, not lecture.

- Provide space and time for quality conversations.[3]

Teens who have parents willing to discuss faith issues will have a stronger chance of living in the Word.

10. Encourage Family Devotions

I don't meet many families who have a devotional time in the Bible or a study in the Scriptures, but the families I have encountered who do have a devotional time have students who are at least curious about the faith.

I met a student at my college who was raised by missionary parents in Thailand. He told me that he and his two brothers had a "Bible hour" five days a week with his dad:

> By the time I was fifteen, I became hard and bitter. I felt forced into reading the Bible. Over the years I would emotionally "leave the building" during my time reading the Bible with my dad and brothers. Now looking back, it was one of the most meaningful times of the week. My parents made me do a lot of things that I didn't want to do that were actually good for me, like brushing my teeth, making my bed, taking a shower, studying for tests, and going to church. Today I am appreciative that my father took time to read the Bible with us.

Bible devotions do not have to be drab or boring. They can be fun if you make them fun. I find there are many odd and weird stories in the

Bible that kids actually want to discuss. Youth workers can help parents by providing resources to engage the heart and mind of their teenager. Consider the simple model called Faith Five, which teaches a family to ask two questions: what was the high of your day and what was the low of your day? A Bible verse is read, then each person is asked what the passage means for their day, and then a blessing is prayed over family members.

Grassroots Transformation

The goal is more than biblical information. We teach and train for life change. Metamorphosis is the process of being changed, like a caterpillar to a butterfly. A new species of being.

What if youth ministry was the grassroots catalyst to change the entire church when it comes to biblical literacy, retention, application, and creativity?

We all know the Sunday morning church service needs a major overhaul. The Sunday morning sermon in "big church" is in dire need of renovation. We need an entire makeover.

Teaching the Bible is more than entertainment and funny lessons. It is so much more than just giving out Bible trivia. It is not just information, but transformation. That's what we want. Let's make a dent in biblical illiteracy by effectively teaching and training folk in God's word.

There is an ancient proverb that says, "Give a man a fish, and you will feed him for a day. Teach a man to fish, and you will feed him for a lifetime."

Let's get it right.

Voices from the Trenches

"One thing we can do is to ask youth better questions in order to understand what they think about God. In a recent Bible study with thirteen-year-old 'church kids,' instead of asking, 'Does God forgive all sins?' I gave them a list of sins and asked them to circle the sins they believed that God *does not* forgive, such as murder, cheating, gossip, premarital sex, stealing, and so on. Everyone circled something, and one girl circled all the sins, except gossiping. When I asked why, she said, 'Well, gossiping doesn't seem that bad. Everyone does it.' We used this discussion as a memorable moment that helped us look more deeply into the Scriptures, which led to a whole new set of great questions."

—Karen, professor of youth ministry, family, and culture

Q's to Experience

1. What are some practical ways to help your kids experience the Scriptures?

2. How does knowing the Bible help someone live out his or her faith? What are some intended outcomes to help students experience the word of God?

3. Why do you think our American youth ministries are scripturally ignorant and allergic to the Bible?

Notes

1. Kara Powell and Chap Clark, *Sticky Faith: Everyday Ideas to Build Lasting Faith in Your Kids* (Grand Rapids, MI: Zondervan, 2011), 71.
2. Ibid.
3. Ibid., 72–88.

Chapter Nine

GRADUATES
WIPEOUT AFTER HIGH SCHOOL

"I don't know if I can make it in the real world."
—Dana, recent high school graduate

Seniors in high school are pretty nervous.

Many seniors will move on to college, some will head into the marketplace, and others will enlist in the armed forces. Seniors are feeling the pressure of performing well on SAT tests and getting into the best universities. Along with this pressure is the feeling of how does God fit into the equation in their next season of life.

In their book *Sticky Faith: Everyday Ideas to Build Lasting Faith in Your Kids*, researchers Kara Powell and Chap Clark point out that only one in seven graduating seniors feels prepared for college.[1] I am certain that most student ministries are not helping seniors transition well to life after high school, and the data shows it.

What's the Problem?

I am not fond of statistics because the numbers for those who drift after high school and for those who don't come and go, but I am a student of trends. It doesn't take a rocket scientist (or a brilliant youth worker) to see that, following high school, a large number of students really struggle with staying committed and alive in their faith. What's gone wrong?

New-found freedom. Our students will graduate from high school, and for the first time many will be free of the rules and the warm TLC of Mom or Dad. No one is telling them what to do. They can skip college classes or miss church if they choose. They have freedom to play and party!

The safety net of church or youth group is finished. Millions of eighteen-to twenty-year-olds will not return to the church and will "graduate from God." For those who had a good or great church experience, now that seems like a distant dream of the past. It's time to start brand-new for the high school graduate.

Poor exiting. Meanwhile the youth ministry has done a "good-bye Sunday" and maybe a "graduation Sunday," which are nice ways to honor and celebrate seniors graduating but lack significant substance and any sustaining power or impact. We have not prepared our seniors well for a new life outside high school.

High anxiety. Students are anxious about the future, and they don't feel ready for life after high school. Seniors are aware of the stress and worry of leaving high school and moving onto the next phase of "young adulthood."

Graduating from God. Seniors are not the only ones worried about moving to the next phase and stage of their lives. Parents are concerned if their kids will study hard and become productive citizens, and youth workers are wondering if students will leave their faith when they graduate from high school.

Will the church engage with these seniors and help them succeed at the next level?

Problem #9 of American Youth Ministry:
Students aren't ready for life after high school.

Finding a Solution

I witnessed a beautiful moment last summer at our church's vacation Bible school (VBS). Our church does VBS well. We have three different venues: morning, afternoon, and evening sessions. We have seen over sixteen hundred kids from the community attend and be impacted. What I saw convinced me of a powerful truth: teens can lead and serve and do it well!

One junior was portraying Jesus and had to memorize his words in John 18–20. By the end of the day of acting out Jesus in the crucifixion, he told me, "I have been crucified thirteen times today." Another sophomore gave me a hug and told me he had been at VBS for twelve hours, saying, "It is a good tired."

Five other high school students were in skits involving stories of the crucifixion and resurrection, eight middle school students were leading crafts, four freshmen were leading outdoor games, and six seniors were doing Bible lessons. Twelve middle school and high school students were leading music and skits.

If we want to stop the spiritual drifting following high school, servanthood and leading are the best remedies and antidotes to this ongoing problem of students falling apart following high school.

Solution to Enlist:
Groom students to learn and lead.

Enlisting students in middle school, high school, and college to learn and lead is a daunting task but exciting to consider. Why are so many of our teens bored? We have failed in capitalizing on developing students into leaders. This chapter helps empower a strategy for students influencing "others." We have pacified teens to death or created the blank stare. We need to give students a large vision that has risk and a cost. We need to help students learn and lead, and here are ten possibilities of getting it right.

Failure through Long-Term Nurture

My observation of thirty-plus years working in youth ministry is that we nurture students to death. What I mean is that we tend to spoon-feed them spiritually so that they don't have to think deeply and critically. One of my friends offers a three-week series for seniors called "Skeptics Night Out." He challenges the youth and encourages healthy debate, questions, and doubts about the Christian faith.

David Kinnaman states in *You Lost Me: Why Young Christians Are Leaving Church—and Rethinking Faith*, "About one out of every nine young Christians (11 percent) said that college experiences caused them to doubt their faith."[2] Allow your students to ask hard questions because if they ever hit the university, I guarantee there will be people of all kinds of philosophies and ideologies that will spin their heads.

Voices from the Trenches

"I believe the key to keeping students from checking out on the church is to not check out on them as seniors. Putting a high emphasis on keeping seniors connected through service and intentional leadership opportunities is paramount. I cannot remember anything my youth pastor ever said in a program talk. What I do remember is her allowing me to lead worship as a young guitar player. I was allowed to succeed and fail, and that was the very thing that helped me grow and stay committed to my faith. Combining student involvement and involvement in the church as a whole—and not just in the student ministry—is the best recipe for a student being committed for the long haul."

—Trevor, paid youth pastor

Recognize Transition Issues

Parents and youth leaders need to be aware of the tremendous pressure for a young adult to leave home and start new. It is easy to forget our first weeks after high school, so be aware of the newness and excitement the post-graduate will be facing. They will also experience some losses: leaving behind friendships, perhaps a dating breakup, and for many, leaving home. The good news for those who attend college close to home is they can go back home to do their laundry and have Mom make homemade chocolate chip cookies.

Determine Intended Outcomes

Jason Lamb of Grace Fellowship Church argues that most youth ministries rarely think through what we want students to know and do by the time they graduate. He has taken time with his team to ask five hard questions:

- What does a student who graduates from our student ministry look like?

- What have they accomplished and done?

- What content have they been exposed to? (What do we want them to know?)

- What experiences do we want every student to have access to?

- What do we want them to be and do fifteen years from now?

A healthy youth ministry will ask, "What are we trying to do with these students?" by the time they graduate. What will they be like? What do we want them to know? What are the intended outcomes we desire for our students?

Create Avenues of Ownership for Seniors

Youth pastors have told me it's hard to keep seniors involved in youth ministry their last year of high school. I think this relates to the transitional issues mentioned above. I actually find it a bit refreshing when seniors in high school spread their wings and spend time away from youth ministry their last year. It is part of the process of leaving the nest. These seniors are ready to move out of youth group, and I think that can be really healthy.

In the meantime, create a place for seniors. I have hosted an event named SOME (Seniors Only Monday Event). We hang out, sometimes go serve at a soup kitchen, or go watch a football game and eat wings. It is a time when the seniors feel affirmed and "special." Most of all, it is hang time for relationships.

Keep Them Involved in "Big Church"

In my experience, most youth workers have trouble getting middle and high school students to attend "big church" with any regularity. Attendance in big church may not be valued highly by students, yet studies suggest it has a huge effect on their spiritual outcomes. Kara Powell and Chap Clark's extensive research led to this startling statement: "There is a relationship between attendance at church-wide worship services and sticky faith."[3]

Involvement in "big church" somehow is linked with growing and maturing faith. There is an intergenerational element, corporate singing, and a biblical challenge that can inspire and create spiritual commitments and movement for seniors in high school that will impact their future.

Voices from the Trenches

"This issue is much bigger than a youth ministry problem. The church needs to rethink its vision for youth ministry and create ways to let students have a sense of ownership now. Almost every adult within the church should be asking the question *How can I invest my time and energy in the younger generation?* It isn't just the youth leaders' responsibility to do ministry with teenagers; it is the responsibility of the entire church. Teenagers have to figure out their role in the church before they graduate from high school."

—Brent, paid youth worker

Keep Their Hearts Tender with Serving Children

Kara Powell and Chap Clark cite one finding about serving little kids that makes lots of sense to me: "Students who serve and build relationships with younger children also tend to have stickier faith."[4]

Don't you love those videos of your seniors hugging a little child? Seniors in high school who serve and lead have a greater chance of continuing with the discipline of serving when they spread their wings and go off to college or wherever they are headed. Serving children builds a deep well of faith for high school students.

Visit College Ministries Sooner Rather Than Later

It isn't unusual or surprising for most seniors graduating from high school to struggle finding a church or campus ministry. I think it is vital to collect data on the college they'll be attending. So find out where the best churches and ministries are for college students.

Finding a church they connect with is no small challenge. I have done college trips with my seniors and helped them meet people from ministries on campus and churches that were both college oriented and intergenerational. Parents and youth pastors need to collaborate on helping seniors find a church. Some churches even take juniors and seniors in high school on college road trips. The goal is that we want our students walking with God for the long haul. I would encourage a simple newsletter to parents titled "Helping Your Senior Find a Great Church in their First Forty Days on Campus." Youth pastors can do some homework on this: create a list of your state colleges and then list a handful of churches and campus ministries (like Campus Crusade, Navigators, Campus Outreach, etc.) for parents and their students to consider.

Prepare High School Seniors with an Exit Strategy

Mt. Horeb United Methodist Church in Lexington, South Carolina, has been offering a five-week senior seminar for those intentionally heading to college. Some of the exit strategy topics are:

- How to deal with an agnostic or atheistic roommate, friend, or professor

- How to find a church and campus ministry

- Management skills: money, time, extracurricular, classes, studying, and friendships

- Spiritual disciplines such as prayer and Bible study

- Navigating friendships and dating boundaries

Voices from the Trenches

"Helping high school seniors not graduate from their faith begins before the final semester of their high school career. Only God knows how long we will have a teen in our ministries, but we must start when kids are in the sixth grade, building into them a foundation of faith that will stay with them well into their adult years. This requires a long-term strategic plan covering important topics of our faith in Jesus. I believe apologetic principles (defending the faith) are absolutely essential as many high school seniors head off to secular universities that will challenge their faith. Our faith is reasonable, and our graduates need to know why and own it when they head out the doors into the real world. Finally, staying in close contact with graduates, and especially in the first month of college when many decisions and relationships are established, is important for their transition to be successful."

—Jeff, pastor of local outreach

Seniors Need Coaching about the "Real World" and Reentry into "Big Church"

It is no surprise that many students, after graduating from high school and then college, also "graduate" from "big church" and move onto other things, sometimes atheism, agnosticism, or sleeping in on Sunday morning. David Kinnaman writes, "The ages eighteen to twenty-nine are the black hole of church attendance; this age segment is 'missing in action from most congregations…about eight million twenty somethings who were active churchgoers as teenagers who will no longer be particularly engaged in a church by their thirtieth birthday."[5]

Keep the Local Church Involved Long Distance

We expect parents to stay connected with their kids when they leave the parental home front, but what about the church? Many seniors have told me, "When I went to college, I felt ignored by the church, almost invisible." What can the church do for those who have left high school?

- Churches can occasionally provide care packages with food and money. Who doesn't like a surprise package?

- Visit them. Take trips to colleges to connect with your graduates.

- Offer gatherings for those locally who don't attend college.

- Host events over Christmas when college kids are home for a week.

- Send a handwritten letter instead of sending an e-mail using social media. Letters are personal and few write them anymore.

- Send e-mail blasts with an encouraging Scripture.

- Follow up and keep connected. Life after high school can be a horrific time of alienation and loneliness. Some students feel disconnected from their faith community.

- We need to "help young adults do something with their faith in order to contextualize their doubts within the church's mission."[6]

Let's change the outcome of seniors in high school. We need to get this one right by grooming students to learn and lead, and if this happens, there is a great chance of their being ready for post–high school living.

Voices from the Trenches

"As a high school student, I know from personal experience that there are specific actions leaders can take to help seniors not lose their faith after high school. Leaders must emphasize the importance of an 'All In' lifestyle for Jesus. Too many high school students have a sectional faith, one in which they do not want Jesus to touch certain parts of their lives, whether that is a relationship with a friend or what they do alone when no one is watching. Without a sold-out faith, high school students will fall away once they hit the temptations of the college and working years."

—Wesley, high school student

Q's to Enlist

1. What is your youth ministry doing to transition your seniors out of high school?

2. What is one practical step your church can take to help seniors get ready to leave high school?

3. What can the church do to walk with graduates of high school?

Notes

1. Kara Powell and Chap Clark, *Sticky Faith: Everyday Ideas to Build Lasting Faith in Your Kids*, (Grand Rapids, MI: Zondervan, 2011), 151.

2. David Kinnaman, *You Lost Me: Why Young Christians Are Leaving Church—and Rethinking Faith* (Grand Rapids, MI: Baker Books, 2011), 188.

3. Powell and Clark, *Sticky Faith*, 97.

4. Ibid., 98.

5. Kinnaman, *You Lost Me*, 22.

6. Ibid., 197.

Chapter Ten

WHY ADULTS AND TEENS NEED EACH OTHER

"REWARD: Lost dog. Three legs, blind in left eye, right ear missing, tail broken, recently neutered. Answers to the name Lucky."
—from a newspaper classified ad

Is youth ministry like the lost dog mentioned above—a bit beat-up with a broken tail but goes by the name Lucky?

American youth ministry has been really lucky (blessed) to have some fabulous adults to work with students. Part of our brokenness is that we keep trying to involve cool, young, hip college kids to be mentors, but what about the older generation (Grandma and Grandpa's generation), the wise sages who have tons of experience and wisdom they can pour into young people?

What's gone wrong? Youth ministry needs to stop choosing *only* young adults, who tend to become overcommitted and irresponsible. They just aren't that reliable; not to mention developmentally they are too close to teenagers' stage of development. There are lots of other groups available to minister to young people.

What's the Problem?

Adolescence is the process of moving away from childhood into adulthood and is a transitional time of life. Whether you consider this seven-year process "heaven or hell on earth," there is one common denominator to this season of life: friendships. Teens spend an enormous amount of time with their peers. Take for example a student attending public or private school who leaves early in the morning by car or bus and spends up to seven hours at the middle or high school. If the student is also involved in sports or extracurricular events, then add on another two to three hours a week plus night games or weekend events. If they are involved in a church youth group, Fellowship of Christian Athletes, or Young Life, then add another three or four hours.

Some folk are against a separate, autonomous gathering of teenagers under the umbrella of church. *I am for youth groups totally, but not to the exclusion of significant adults.*

I see nothing wrong with students who want to be with their friends first and foremost because I know peer friendship is the glue of teenage culture. Friends are a needed component for adolescents. For an adult to want to hang around teens could be perceived as weird, and I understand that. But where I want the church to step up and make a stand is on adults and teens doing some life and faith issues together.

We need to make sure youth ministry creates an intergenerational model of older mentors, who have experienced the ups and downs of life and the hard knocks of being human, connecting with young people. Whatever happened to senior citizens and the elderly in the church doing more than handing out bulletins?

Problem #10 of American Youth Ministry:
Youth ministry is too age segregated and devoid of significant adult influences.

I took one of my youth ministry classes to Starbucks a few weeks ago and asked them to watch people while we had coffee and discussed the topic of this chapter: why teens and adults need each other. "Look and see if you notice any teenagers and adults coming in together?"

Over the course of two hours, none of us observed any teenagers hanging out with an adult. Our culture just seems to shy away from it, deeming it strange or odd.

I have heard key figures in the Christian community say that there should never be a set-apart meeting of teenagers. Videos and documentaries such as *Divided* articulate that "youth ministry is not biblical," and some assert "youth ministry is antibiblical."

I would agree that "youth ministry is not biblical," as children's ministry, singles ministry, music styles, worship bulletins, multi-sites for worship, baptismal pools, church organs, podcasts, Twitter, church buses, use of technology, and church secretaries are not biblical.

Yes, it is true that the term or idea of *youth ministry* is not biblical, namely because youth ministry is a twentieth-century invention for a serious need. But to say that youth ministry is *antibiblical* is going way too far over the edge. When people say that youth ministry is a "dangerous threat" to the church, I could not disagree more wholeheartedly. I have met thousands of teens who have come to faith in Jesus Christ *because* of youth ministry. I have personally led hundreds of students to faith in Jesus and have spoken at camps, conferences, and retreats, in which teens stood to follow Jesus as Savior and follow him as Lord. Some have surrendered to vocational Christian ministry, and others have chosen to be a faithful witness in the marketplace or overseas in missions.

One time a graduate student asked me, "Would you rather kill off youth ministry and just lump all congregational members together?" My answer was then and still is: "No. Are you kidding me?" I view youth ministry as extremely vital, necessary, and integral to the life of the church. I believe teens need their space and place to worship and hang out, but not alone with peers all the time.

Finding a Solution

It doesn't take a rocket scientist to see that teenagers in America are isolated from adults. American youth ministry is high on teenage relationships and pretty devoid of significant adults relating to teenagers.

Most public and private schools have medium to large classes with one teacher and an assistant, and the homeschool movement has made strides to get their students out of the house and into the community with other peers and adults.

Teens are isolated from the adult world. Many adults either are afraid of teens or think, "Teens don't want to be with us." Some folk believe adults have generally abandoned our young.

Our churches have very little interaction with teens and adults together, and my contention is that the worship service of most American congregations doesn't do a good job of integration. American youth ministry has become segregated by age. Some churches actually discourage teens from being in "big church" because the topics discussed might be thought by some to be age-inappropriate, and so youth are strongly encouraged to attend youth-only services. Why we continue to separate teens and adults is baffling.

Think how autonomous we have become. American youth groups tend to have their own budgets, mission trips, and worship teams and small groups. We have youth camps and youth conferences, and that is the good news—students are involved in the gospel. The bad news is that most of these "successful" student ministries are lacking adults.

I am grateful that more and more churches are requiring two adults for every youth group event. Some churches have gone so far as to cancel an event if there are not enough adults present. Adults and teenagers need each other.

Solution to Embrace:
Move to more intergenerational ministry.

Let's Affirm That Teens Need Space and a Place

There's a movement that suggests that all age groups should be together in worship and that there shouldn't be age-segregated classes or groups. Some churches refuse to ever break up into age groups. *No nurseries?*

There is something inside me that really likes the concept of the "whole family" worshiping together, but I think we also need not disregard what we can learn from the social sciences, psychology, learning styles, and brain development.

Yes, there is great value in a family who "prays together [and] stays together." There is also a developmental truth that teens need autonomy, which is short for saying, "Give me a car." Autonomy is the need to have some independence, some space, and individuation.

The homeschool movement is a strong proponent of removing age segregation not only for families but also in church life. There are many strong and viable reasons to like what homeschoolers have to say, and yet I am not hearing them say teenagers need autonomy to hang out with their peers. They believe youth group is nonbiblical and counterproductive.

At the time puberty kicks in, some hormonal changes happen. One of the distinct traits of a teenager is wanting independence. As adolescence emerges and expands, teens want new "natives" and new faces at their table. That would include friends, teachers, coaches, neighbors, and other influencers. Let's acknowledge that young people need space and autonomy. Forcing a young person to meet only with adults in a congregational setting and to keep them away from peers is ridiculous, insidious, and ultimately precarious to the young person. Why? A teen's identity is wrapped up in peer friendships, and to take that away is like cutting off a teen's oxygen. Friendship is the glue in adolescent culture. Adolescents need privacy, with their own space and a place to hang out.

Don't Build a Youth "Ghetto"

If you are hearing me fight *for* independence, you are correct. What I am fighting *against* in American youth ministry is creating a "youth ghetto," meaning a group of teenagers who are constantly off to themselves on a "spiritual island" away from the rest of the members. This youth ghetto is not advantageous; in fact, it is antithetical to spiritual and emotional growth.

Teens need adults and adults need teens. Mark DeVries says, "Family-based youth ministry accesses the incomparable power of the nuclear family and connects students to an extended family of Christian adults to the end that those students grow toward maturity in Christ."[1]

Voices from the Trenches

"Modern youth ministry, in which adults and teens are separated from each other most of the time, is neither healthy nor productive. Segregating adults and teens isn't working."

—Sam, professor of youth ministry, family, and culture

Teens Need Adults as Mentors

American youth groups need more people at the table besides one or two cool and hip college students. One of the greatest sages of my ministry was Nip Slaughter, now deceased. Nip came on board on my youth ministry team at the age of fifty-five. Nip was not a Bible scholar, and to my knowledge he never took a theology class or attended a seminar on "understanding teenagers."

Nip became one of the greatest volunteer leaders I have ever had in my almost three decades of student ministry. He was wise and a great listener, and the kids felt safe with him. A great volunteer team will have diversity: a single mom or dad, some couples, and parents; and please add some folk in their fifties, sixties, and seventies. One volunteer—we call her Miss Mary—is eighty-two years old and helps cook for our church outreach called Fifth Quarter, which serves food after the local football games on Friday night. Fifth Quarter is an event directed toward high school students and occurs on Friday nights after local football games, as an alternative to dangerous partying and other negative influences. Miss Mary is a welcome and valuable addition to this event.

Voices from the Trenches

"The church desperately needs to reclaim a multigenerational vision. Titus 2 provides a God-ordained method for passing faith to succeeding generations. The question today is, 'How will we as a church intentionally create time and space to make this happen?' It may mean simplifying our calendars. It may mean transforming the programs we have to include interaction among generations. It may mean ending some programs that keep youth and children isolated from the larger family. It will be hard to dismiss the younger generations when they are worshiping alongside us on Sunday mornings. We must do whatever is necessary to align our ministries and reflect on what we are leaving behind."

—Andrew, paid youth worker

Adults Need Teens for Spontaneity and Creativity

In the same way that teens need wisdom and guidance from wise older sages, adults need to be around young people. Middle school and high school students have incredible freedom to be spontaneous and creative. One of the developmental milestones of aging is settling down, paying off a house, and being an empty nester.

Men and women who are climbing the ladder in years can be negative, critical, and cynical at times. Teenagers can help those who are further up the ladder to dream, set, goals, and create new bucket lists.

"The importance of adult volunteers involved with youth ministry cannot be stressed enough. Most adults are wiser and have experienced the temptations that we as high school students face on a daily basis. In my life, many adults (of all ages) have helped me when I have had doubts and have been there when I needed to admit my sin. When I struggled with stuff, the adults in my life helped me face the temptation and break free of the sin pattern that had consumed my life. It is so important to have quality, strong adults in a teenager's life."

—Wesley, high school student

Teens and Senior Citizens Have More Commonality Than You Realize

The population of senior citizens is growing to over thirty million in America. There are a number of similarities between teens and those who are aging, for example, loneliness, the need for connection, isolationism, and comparing oneself with others. Teenagers and older adults are asking the question, "Am I making any kind of difference?" We not only need each other but also can teach each other many lessons about life. Self-worth is not just an adolescent issue; it is a thorn in the side of many senior citizens.

Teenage Isolationism Is Not Healthy in the Church

Human beings don't do well in isolation. In fact, God created us to be in relationship and community. God told the two first humans in Genesis 2:18: "It's not good for the Man to be alone; I'll make him a helper, a companion" (*The Message*).

A number of youth workers have commented that in a "church service" setting—for example, in a balcony area designed for "the youth group"—when no adults are present, the behavior is typically childish and extremely immature. But throw a few adults and parents into the balcony and you wonder what just happened. All of a sudden the giggling and belching and texting and sleeping and leaving disappear. The presence of adults changes the landscape of adolescent behavior. Every ministry must find workable models that incorporate parents, teens, and adults in order to heighten Christian discipleship. It is impossible for a teen to develop spiritual maturity and spiritual health without the influence of the extended family of adults called "the church."

Senior Citizens Can Do More Than Hand Out Bulletins

I think it is neat when church groups of folk who are over sixty years old get together for meals and take sightseeing trips. I have heard of groups, with names such as "39 and Holding" and "Over-the-Hill Gang," who want to do more than take excursions to museums and to the opening of a new zoo. Senior citizens still want to make an impact, and the way for this to happen is for someone to create *environments* to get these teens and senior citizens together.

I am convinced that teenagers cannot grow to their full potential without rubbing shoulders with adults, and I know that senior citizens have tons of wisdom, insight, and experiences of a lifetime to share with teenagers and have stories to tell!

Voices from the Trenches

"One of the best volunteers that I have ever had was a sweet lady in her eighties. She had such spiritual wisdom and such a love to lead young girls in their faith! She began working with a high school girls' small group, and over time she began to lead the group. It gave me such joy to see a sixteen-year-old girl walking together with this woman after church because they were going to get lunch together. This happened often. It was her joy to cook with them, teach them the Bible, and send them handwritten notes on a regular basis. She offered them more than just wisdom; she learned to listen to them and pray for them earnestly. These girls began to really seek out her wisdom because they trusted her. Also, she wasn't afraid to be all in. We had her participate in funny videos, and she even danced to a rap song at one point. Her age was never an issue to the students, because they loved her heart for Jesus and her desire to be a part of their lives."

—Grace Marie, paid youth worker

The Church Is an Extended Family for Teens and Adults

My friend Mark DeVries told me that youth ministry is like an orphanage. Youth culture does not provide or carry its members through life. That is why teens hanging out only with teens can be an unhealthy equation. There will not be fully fledged maturity when teens are left alone.

The body of Christ has untapped power of all age groups and life stages and can have enormous influence on youth. Christianity is about, more than anything, connection and pulling together these various groups to maximize life experiences.

There will be no growth without it.

Go Radical: Reduce "Island" Time

Teens are not children, nor are they adults; but they are emerging into adults. Timothy recognized this and did something that almost split his church and might have cost him his job. For years Timothy was locked into three meetings a week—Sunday school, Sunday night, and Wednesday night—with very little room for change.

Over the course of time and after being influenced by Doug Fields's *Purpose-Driven Youth Ministry*, Timothy recognized that most of the teens in attendance were the same students at all three events and some of the adult volunteers were the same as well. So Timothy had a heart-to-heart talk with his pastor and convinced him to reduce the number of meetings from three to two. The problem was this: what does the church do for those who insist that some program should still be available for their kids on Sunday night?

Timothy and his pastor came up with a brilliant idea. Their church building was next door to an assisted living community with more than one hundred elderly people in residence.

The idea was simple: those students who wanted "youth group" would need to come up with a ministry plan to "hang out" with the elderly. They could come weekly, once a month, once a year, or whatever their hearts desired. The bottom line is that after taking one event a week off the calendar and reducing the number of meetings and stress load on Timothy, the students have a ministry opportunity working with the elderly. Oh, by the way, Sunday night at the assisted living community has the biggest attendance of the week for this youth ministry, and students are engaging in deep conversation with some of the residents at the assisted living community.

> ## Voices from the Trenches
>
> "Throughout the Bible, we are given instructions and examples of older believers pouring their lives into the younger believers. The more mature in Christ invest in those who are coming up in Christ. Like the Israelites telling stories to their younger community members, we need the older generations sharing stories of God's power and purpose. Like Paul investing in Timothy, older believers in Christ need to come alongside through the power of the Holy Spirit to share not just information but their lives with the younger generations. This has been God's plan through the ages and has to be the center of our ministries to teens."
>
> —Jeff, pastor of local outreach

Let the Church Embrace Diversity

We have read the studies of students being integrated into the life of the body of Christ. "Big church" attendance is important, but one of the hidden secrets that has long-term sustainability is *relationships with all ages*.

My understanding of the church is multigenerational: the young hanging out with older folk and worshiping together with people who are different from me. Mike Yaconelli said it well: "Youth group is good. But there's a better good. It's called church. Not youth church, or contemporary church, or postmodern church. Just plain, boring, ordinary church."[2]

It does not require large budgets to get adults mingling with and investing into the next generation. It just takes leadership, vision, and time. One of the most important priorities a congregation can have is creating environments in which teens meet with older men and women, in which spontaneous learning and teaching emerge.

This is the church at its best: old and young, having coffee together, singing songs, and praying for one another.

Let's go one step further toward what the kingdom is all about: being multiethnic. American churches (and youth groups) are also racially segregated. Revelation 7:9 speaks of life after this life and worshiping around the throne of God: "From every nation, tribe, people and language."

Imagine heaven: all people groups, all colors represented, all praising the King of Kings and Lord of Lords. Every tribe and language will be present. Oh what a day that will be!

143

So, back to planet earth for a moment. Let's rethink the process of getting ready for heaven now, starting with the power of integration—just plain, boring, ordinary church.

Would you take a moment and pray the prayer Jesus taught us: "Your kingdom come, your will be done, *on earth as it is in heaven*" (emphasis mine).

Voices from the Trenches

"In some ways this is true of youth ministry, that we have become too age segregated and separate from the church. I believe it is the reason that many teens leave the church after they graduate from high school. After the fun programming is over, they are left with almost zero connection to the church. A goal we must have as youth ministry is showing teens how they fit into 'big church' now. Part of this process is assimilating them into the church during their middle and high school years."

—Brent, paid youth worker

Q's to Embrace

1. How has your group become isolated from the rest of the church?

2. What are some practical steps you can take to become more intergenerational?

3. Think of one or two senior adults whom you can invite to share their experiences on a panel discussion.

Notes

1. Mark DeVries, *Family-Based Youth Ministry* (Downers Grove, IL: InterVarsity Press, 2004), 176.

2. Wayne Rice, *Reinventing Youth Ministry (Again): From Bells and Whistles to Flesh and Blood* (Downers Grove, IL: InterVarsity Press, 2010), 187.

Chapter Eleven

FAMILY MATTERS
MORE THAN A YOUTH WORKER

"I got into this gig thinking I would only be working with kids. I had no idea
this was a family thing."
—Burt, paid youth leader, twenty-six years old

Sherry attended our youth retreat and spent the entire weekend hearing about God's desire to have a relationship with us. On Saturday evening, she became a follower of Jesus. She was radiant. Glowing. Alive. When our group returned to the church building on Sunday, many parents were there to pick up their children, but Sherry waited an hour. When a pickup truck came barreling into the parking lot, her countenance changed from joy to a look of disappointment—almost melancholy. Sherry climbed into her dad's truck, stared straight ahead, and left in a cloud of dust.

Two weeks passed. Sherry hadn't come to any group meetings. I asked some students if they knew what was going on. "Sherry's parents won't let her come back to youth group anymore," they reported. "Why?" I asked. They said, "Her parents don't believe in religious stuff."

At that point I began to understand that the group with the most impact on teenagers isn't youth workers, pastors, or other teens; it's their families.

What's the Problem?

As much as we love to work with students, youth ministry will be limited if we exclude working with families. Our tradition paradigm won't have staying power if we focus only on the island of youth ministry. We will have the greatest impact on teens' present and their future by leveraging our influence toward helping families.

We have a few choices: we can ignore families and settle on ministering only to students, or we can seek to help families become healthy and balanced.

Problem #11 of American Youth Ministry:

The traditional paradigm of student ministry as an island limits the ministry's power to transform.

If we focus only on teenagers, it's like focusing on only one piece of the puzzle, yet there are other pieces of the puzzle besides the adolescent. I cannot expect to help a student long-term if I ignore the family, and that is why understanding family systems is so important to youth workers. A family system is a husband, wife, children, and the past three to seven generations in the families of both the husband and wife.

Family systems theory asserts that the whole is greater than the sum of the parts. Families consist of individuals who are interconnected and interrelated. There are a variety of systems in life. Our body is a system. The church is a system. The universe is a system. Even the government—shutdowns and all—is a system. The same goes for the family. Every system leans toward health (life) or death, and family systems are either open or closed systems. One of our jobs as youth workers is sniffing out where our students are coming from so we can help them for the long haul.

Finding a Solution

Identifying family systems will give you a head start in your understanding of youth ministry. Even more significant than that is that it will help the entire congregation take steps in ministering to the *whole family*. As you work with students, recognize that they are not just individuals, but they have been formed by a *family system* that has rules, values, habits, and attitudes that have shaped them into who they are today.

The teens you are working with come from a system that is usually considered *open* or *closed*. One of the most inspiring moments in my life was witnessing the birth of my children, Rachel, our daughter, and our son, Andrew. These little miracles were wrinkled, slimy, and crying but were very much alive. A newborn is probably the purest example of an open system.

I've worked as a chaplain in cancer wards at hospitals. Men and women in these terminal conditions deteriorate before your eyes; it's gut-wrenching. Nothing seems more tragic. Dying systems. Closed systems.

So how can you tell if the students you come in contact with are from a family system that is living or dying—open or closed? Compare it to five basic characteristics of an open, living family system.

Order. Any business, church, or family that's working and running properly has structure. What happens to a church without policies, orders, and organization? Death happens if the needs of the congregation aren't addressed and met. The same is true for families. An open family system has organization.

Purpose. One of the first tasks of a new company is generating a mission statement, bylaws, objectives, and goals. When a family has direction, vision, and mission, that family is alive. Proverbs 29:18 says, "Where there is no revelation, the people cast off restraint." But when there's no unified purpose or plan, families tend to splinter in different directions.

Adaptability. One of the signs of a dying marriage is resistance to change. Consider the husband and wife who get lost while driving. "Do you realize we're lost?" the wife asks rhetorically. The more she complains, the faster her husband drives. Finally he can't take it anymore and pulls off the road. "Okay, we're lost," he argues. "But at least we're making great time." This scenario reveals that there is some openness to admitting mistakes and changing directions—especially in tougher times than a wayward road trip. We're more likely to see a light at the end of the tunnel and grow in the process.

Openness to Feedback. At the heart of an open family system is communication and trust. Organizations tend to prosper when they promote feedback and constructive criticism. The same is true with families. When family members tell each other the truth and share feelings, it indicates that their family's vital signs are working and healthy.

Ability to Resolve Conflict. Conflict is inevitable in any system simply because systems are composed of different, interconnected parts. When there's a breakdown in the system—even in one part—confusion and chaos often result. Family members who trust each other, however, try for resolutions to problems. But conflict resolution is rarely part of a dysfunctional family. The members usually don't have the skills and coping mechanisms necessary to effectively handle issues.

Solution to Enhance:

The future of youth ministry is the entire church ministering to the whole family.

Helping Families

Determining a family system's degree of openness will tell you a lot about the family's health. We need to admit that we are called to do more than just babysit teenagers in a spiritual environment. We are called to so much more!

It doesn't take long to recognize that there are many hurting and dysfunctional families (Christian and non-Christian). In this chapter, I will identify five family systems we are working with: *rigid, chaotic, disengaged, enmeshed,* and *balanced.* The ultimate goal is for the entire church to help families move toward a healthy and balanced life.

If you take a casual journey through the Bible, starting with the book of Genesis, you will soon discover that following Adam and Eve's sin, all families begin to struggle in life. Since the fall all homes have been plagued with brokenness and sin. Part of the role of the church is to help families through the power of Jesus regain some level of wholeness in this lifetime.

So we start to scan beneath the surface and look at five family systems that you will face as a youth leader. The first two—the rigid and chaotic family systems—concern the issue of *adaptability* (how well the family responds to change and stress). The next two—the disengaged and enmeshed systems—focus more on *attachments* (if the family relationships are too close or too distant and if they emotionally bond or disconnect). The fifth and last model is the balanced family system, which is able to adjust and grow in health and a balanced approach to relationships.

The Rigid Family

A character in the movie *Dead Poets Society* (1989) is a teenage boy who has discovered the joys of theater and is confronted severely by his rigid father. The father is displeased with his son's "rebellion" (which is more adolescent individuation than overt anarchy) and basically says, "You're not going to ruin your life. I'm withdrawing you from school and enrolling you in a military academy. You are going to Harvard, and you are going to be a doctor!" The atmosphere becomes so oppressive and judgmental that the boy has no energy left to battle his father. The boundaries are too rigid. He can't cope any longer. Following their argument, the boy kills himself with his father's pistol.

In a rigid home, there's usually one authoritative leader, whom I call the "benevolent dictator." The subordinates know the rules are tight, often legalistic, and sometimes militaristic. Discipline is harsh and strict. In a rigid home, flexibility and adaptability are nonexistent. But one directive reigns supreme: do what the leader says or suffer the consequences. Since loyalty to the head of the family is intense, kids tend to acquiesce and comply or totally rebel. This kind of system is oppressive to teenagers and sometimes leads to abuse.

If parents maintain high demands in areas such as academics or athletics, children can become paralyzed and afraid. In a rigid family system, kids tend to comply out of fear, not out of love. Parents' high bar of expectations can also lead teens to compulsive, addictive performance orientations. And failure could lead to depression and low self-esteem. As parents keep demanding, children try harder and harder to please them. Eventually children will start resenting their parents' taxing, unrealistic burdens and eventually will shut down. In *Dead Poets Society*, the father intimidates the boy so much and shuts him down so fiercely on an emotional level, the teen goes downstairs, finds his father's pistol, and commits suicide.

The rigid family is *high on rules* and *low on relationships*. How can a youth worker spot a teenager from a rigid home? The warning signs will probably be *depression* and *anxiety*. The goal here is to help the rigid family *loosen the reins* with solid instruction and counseling.

The Chaotic Family

The movie *Mrs. Doubtfire* (1993) is a classic case study on the chaotic family. The boundaries here are unclear, and conflicts have become immovable objects. Robin Williams's character (the dad) and Sally Field's character (the mom) have a sour marriage and are heading for a divorce. Williams's character doesn't know how to lead, and his children are confused about who's in charge—Mom, Dad, or no one.

This family system is at the other end of the *adaptability* pendulum. This chaotic family system has little or no leadership. Family members might discuss problems, but there's confusion over how to solve them, so they are swept under the carpet. A chaotic family system operates impulsively and disciplines children erratically. The boundaries in a chaotic family are blurry and diffused. Children often assert the parental role, taking on responsibilities out of their realm of emotional and mental capabilities. They assume dual roles: son and father, daughter and mother.

The chaotic family system also spawns *infantilization,* in which teens are "demoted" to small-child status. Parents don't treat them like young adults, but as infants. Boundaries in a chaotic home are cyclical and unwritten. For example, a mother and father become Christians when their kids reach adolescence. One evening, out of nowhere, the father says: "Starting tomorrow, we're going to have devotions." The kids respond: "What are devotions?" The family reads the Bible for three days and quits. The chaotic family often has good intentions but not much follow-through. Teens from chaotic families often conclude that decisions in their home weren't made and that they just "happened all of a sudden."

The chaotic family is *high on relationships* and *low on rules,* and nobody is sure who is in charge from day to day. A teenager who lives in a chaotic system will show signs of *distrust* and *confusion.* The task for a healthy church is to help this family discover some boundaries that actually *tighten the reins* and figure out the various roles and rules of the home.

The Disengaged Family

The movie *Ordinary People* (1980) focuses on Timothy Hutton's character who attempts suicide after his older brother drowns in a boating accident. Following the death, the family grows apart, and Hutton and his parents (played by Donald Sutherland and Mary Tyler Moore) show signs of anger, blame, and denial. Like many children in disengaged families lacking emotional closeness, the teenage child exhibits behavioral problems. Most notable is the *identified patient syndrome* (IPS). The identified patient is the family's scapegoat, unfairly bearing problems and consequences and often rebelling through drugs, violence, and truancy. In *Ordinary People,* Hutton's IPS stems from blaming himself for his brother's death.

The disengaged family system *lacks intimacy.* Members seem independent and isolated from one another. If a family member is asked, "Do you love one another?" the answer might be, "Sure. But we're so busy that we don't get much time together." To disengage means to separate, to dissociate. The disengaged family isn't bonded; the members are unplugged, unhooked. Its members lead disconnected lives and hardly know one another on an intimate basis.

There is little loyalty in the disengaged home but plenty of independence and freedom. This might be the number one kind of family in America, for disengaged families are busy families.

In a disengaged home, decisions are made at an individual level. Dinners are rarely eaten together, and family members are constantly coming and going and on different schedules. When considering whether your students are from this type of system, ask them how many minutes they spend in meaningful dialogue with their parents or siblings. Usually there's little interaction. Signs that a teen comes from a disengaged system are *isolation* and *lacking emotion*. This family has become emotionally and relationally disconnected.

A growing healthy church can help counsel this family into *some structural ways of reconnection and communication.*

The Enmeshed Family

Adam Sandler stars in the movie *The Waterboy* (1998). Sandler's character, Bobby Boucher, has a mother (Kathy Bates) who doesn't believe her son. Bobby has the ability to function in life without his "Mama." She's an over-functioning mother who doesn't want her son to have a life on his own or exist without her. "You don't have what they call the social skills," she says, and proceeds, "that's why you don't have any friends, except your Mama."

The enmeshed family system is one of unhealthy closeness. Teens may use words and phrases such as *smothered, suffocating,* or *won't stop calling me on the cell phone* when describing their home lives. An enmeshed person is entangled in a web of relationships with no clear boundaries. Those outside it may assume an enmeshed family is really close. But insiders are probably thinking, *Let me out of here!* The enmeshed family system does not respect boundaries or privacy, so a healthy church can coach family members to *give some space, autonomy, and freedom with some clear guardrails.*

Voices from the Trenches

"A youth worker's role should be to come alongside parents and help with the process of nurturing teenagers. One of the biggest failures in youth ministry has been our lack of partnership with parents in the spiritual formation of their children. The reality we must face is that our time with teenagers is relatively short. We have an incredible opportunity to invest in the lives of teenagers, but it pales in comparison to the investment of a lifelong parent.

"The first step is: the whole church needs to develop a vision for partnering with families. If the church is going to be successful in ministering to families, it is going to take the entire church, not just the youth ministry.

"Second, youth workers need to approach parents much like we approach teenagers. Get to know them, pray for them, and spend time investing in them. A third step would be planning two events a year that specifically targeted parents. Even with a busy youth ministry schedule we could find time to fit that in, especially if the entire church is bought into the vision for ministering to families.

"Scripture teaches that the most influential person in a kid's life is the parent. We have to be willing to change our strategy of youth ministry and be willing to invest in families."

—Brent, paid youth worker

The Balanced Family

Father of the Bride (1991 version) offers the classic balanced family, in which there is laughter, camaraderie, hugging, forgiveness, and flexibility to change. George Banks (played by Steve Martin) learns that his daughter, Annie (Kimberly Williams), is engaged. He goes from denial to anger, then stubbornness, and finally alters his life to a gentle, winsome attitude that allows his daughter to spread her wings (with a big thanks to Mrs. Banks, played by Diane Keaton). This family is about communication, affection, listening, and times to laugh and play.

You might be wondering whether there are *any* balanced families. There are. In fact, even the first four dysfunctional family systems can experience moments of wholeness. But the balanced family stands apart because of *healthy interdependence.* It's become a safe place where members learn the value of clearly defined boundaries. The rules are fair, understood, and consistent. This family system places a high priority on elastic leadership—*pliability* and *adaptability.* The roles are clear—moms are moms, dads are dads, and kids are kids. There is humor, respect, listening, fun, togetherness, service, communication, daily loving affection, shared responsibility, and forgiveness.

The members of a balanced family have grown to appreciate one another. Each is encouraged to grow and develop. Family members can still remain a close bunch without compromising their individuality. The bottom line is that members of a balanced family system can be autonomous without being isolated, attached without being suppressed.

A balanced family is a healthy home. Healthy homes contribute to a balanced and healthy church because the church is made up of families.

The growing healthy church can guide families to go for the benchmark of health and wholeness by *encouraging adaptability and constant communication, affection and biblical conflict resolution.*[1]

A Word to Youth Workers

After studying these family systems, maybe you've come to the conclusion that your family of origin or present family isn't the greatest. Maybe you grew up in a rigid or enmeshed family system and are stuck in the same old patterns. Don't lose hope. How can you help your own system and also encourage other family systems?

1. Start by Uncovering Your Own Family Systems Baggage

This means becoming a student of history—your family history. Ask parents and other relatives about your grandparents and great grandparents. Investigate what made the people in your family tree tick. What past behaviors—negative and positive—have contributed to your attitudes and well-being? Are your parents workaholics? Are you? Check it out. Look for addictions or tendencies in your mother or father that you exhibit. Take a family systems course at a local college.

2. Are You Compassionate or Critical?

Read some books to help you see where you've been so you can heal the wounds you may be carrying. It is hard to minister to others when we are carrying too much baggage. I meet way too many youth workers who are critical of families who don't have it together, and then they start judging families who have addictions that don't seem to go away.

An understanding of family systems will actually produce a sense of compassion for families and a desire to see them heal and mend.

3. Admit Your Own Brokenness

Broken teens need to know that youth workers are breakable. Students want to trust us, but they won't until they see us become *open and vulnerable.*

In my first ever role as a paid youth leader, I was trying to "earn the right to be heard," and for some reason I thought if I told all my success stories of evangelism on airplanes and how I had sold my life out to Jesus that my kids would be impressed. One Sunday night, I was teaching and broke down in tears and talked about how I was struggling to trust God in some area. When the night was over, evidently some kids resonated with my "achy-breaky heart" and stuck around. I noticed Nicky in the back, apparently wanting to be the last person to speak with me.

Nicky came up to me while sheepishly looking at the ground. She said, "David, you have been here for about a year now...[pause] and I have never really liked you." (I am thinking, "Okay, thanks for the encouragement.")

She continued, "It seems like you are trying so hard to electrify us with your perfect Christian life, but I've never found trusting God easy. But tonight when you cried and confessed that being a Christ-follower is hard for you sometimes, I said to myself, 'Tonight, David Olshine has become my youth pastor.' I now can look to you for leadership."

What if our brokenness is actually a gift?

Genesis 3 records the fall of mankind. Adam and Eve sin, and God asks them, "Where are you?" The first humans had an achy-breaky heart. Adam was dealing with emotions of hurt and shame never experienced before, and he explains to God the true state of his heart: "I was afraid, so I hid."

We are all broken, aren't we? We hide and wear masks and pretend we have our acts together. Humans are so complex! Most youth workers on any given day are sincere, loving, and godly, *and* they are insecure, competitive, comparison driven, and annoyed. We are jars of clay, cracked and damaged.

Henry Nouwen calls ministers of Christ "wounded healers," and it has been said Thornton Wilder spoke of "in love's service only the wounded soldiers can serve."

What if all youth workers accepted that we are all wounded soldiers and beaten-up warriors and that "when we are weak, then we are strong, for the power of Christ rests on us? Didn't Jesus say, "Take my body, broken for you?"

What if our messes can be redeeming and healing?

We don't have to hide anymore. We are loved by God. God loves broken youth workers. So when you have a heart that aches, give yourself permission to "come clean." Your soul needs the confession and cleansing, and your students will love you for being real and honest. "In love's service, only the wounded can serve."[2]

Voices from the Trenches

"Helping teenagers in the present in family matters will actually prepare them for the future if they choose to marry and have children. By enhancing students and families with the knowledge of family systems, we are helping teens and the following generations. Working with families is messy but necessary. Too often church programs keep to themselves and do their own thing. We need to connect each ministry from young children to senior citizens, not just isolate groups. The family potluck, during which everyone gathers together, is probably one of the biggest 'wins' the church has ever done."

—Sam, professor of youth ministry, family, and culture

---

4. Focus on Families, Not Just on Teens

Healthy churches should offer regular classes and seminars for all types of family systems for all life stages. Consider just a few of the many groups and accompanying needs many congregations already address:

- Expectant parents

- Parents of elementary children and teens

- Preparing for adolescence

- Engagement discovery weekends

- Mid-life classes

- Handling conflicts

- Money management

- Divorce recovery for parents and recovery for kids and teens from homes of divorce

- Twelve-step programs

- Marriage retreats

- Fourth- through sixth-grade meetings

- Junior high, senior high, and college ministries

- Ministry to senior citizens

- Help for families seeking to adopt or those who have adopted

- Help with blended families

- Teaching couples to pray

- Teaching parents how to talk about God at home

What would it look like if there were fewer "youth programs" and more intentional personal ministry to teens and their families? What would it be like if every youth worker tried to spend time with families rather than look for the latest game for "Messy Night"?

5. Teach about Family Systems

Find someone who can educate you, your staff, and your congregation about issues such as triangles, self-differentiation, over-functioning, under-functioning, and emotional cutoffs. Teens and singles can grasp most of this information, and parents want help in growing as a family.

Remember that we are not just concerned about getting teens through the seven-year adolescent tunnel; we want to see them grow into mature godly people who most likely will become husbands and wives and fathers and mothers and grandparents in the future. That is why the Bible uses the phrase *generation to generations*. We are looking not just to the past or to the present but to the future outcome of the students and families we are working with.

6. Embrace Family Counseling

Most youth workers are scared to counsel teens *and* their parents because several issues such as fear, lack of experience in family counseling, and age differences. This is especially true for single, twenty-something youth workers who have no kids of their own. But regardless of our fears, we should move in the direction of family therapy. I have found that although family counseling isn't needed in every situation, it can enhance the growth of teens and their parents.

Talk with your senior pastor and other staff members about receiving additional training in family counseling skills. It will pay off in the long run. And don't forget to have a list of trusted psychologists, medical staff, legal and law enforcement references, and psychiatrists in the area for referrals and therapy.

Might I add that paid youth workers train volunteers in basic counseling skills or at least provide some training for them. I have lost count of the number of times teens have gone to their Sunday school teacher or small-group leader with a problem and didn't want my "great wisdom." When this happened, as I began ministry years ago, I was hurt, but over the course of years, I actually celebrated when a struggling teenager didn't come to me! It is a great joy when teens go to nonpaid people whom they trust; therefore, it is important that we provide the tools and resources to make it happen for our volunteers.

Here is the final word on counseling: take some of your core students on a Saturday getaway and teach them basic listening skills so they can minister to their friends who are struggling. Trust me on this, there will be times when the only person a teenager will trust is a peer, so it's vital that some of our students know the guidelines on confidentiality, when to listen, when to give advice, and how to refer.

7. Know When to Refer

Youth workers need other people from the helping professions at the table. How does one know when to refer? I like to use an acrostic called REFER:

R—Refer when in over your head. If you are dealing with an area that is way beyond your expertise, find the people who work best in that area (drugs addiction counselors, or sexual or domestic abuse counselors).

E—Establish boundaries. That means it's okay to say to a teen or a family, "I know of someone who is super qualified to help you with this area—much more than I am." Remember that boundaries are the ability to know who we are and who we are not! If the problem exceeds your knowledge or you've taken the persons involved as far as you can lead them, refer and let it go.

F—Find specialists. On my phone are over a half dozen people who, with a quick text or push of a button, are referral experts in my area and who know students and families and are more knowledgeable than I on such issues as addictions and other struggles.

E–Encourage support. One of the main jobs as youth leaders is to encourage and support ongoing growth and healing. Just because we refer our students to someone else does not mean we abdicate words of affirmation and loving support.

R–Resist the Messiah complex. It is constantly tempting to believe that we can help anybody and everybody, but in reality, we cannot, so give up the chance to be the Messiah. There is only one God, and it is not us.

Voices from the Trenches

"Allow teens more time at home instead of constantly being brought to the youth room. I once had a parent tell me that she felt more like a chauffeur for her kids rather than a parent. She would go from one sporting event to another, to music lessons, and then to youth events. Youth ministries aren't necessarily to blame for this, because there are tons of things competing for students' time and commitment. However, we do need to be aware of time issues instead of contributing to the problem."

—Grace Marie, paid youth worker

---

8. Organize Family-Based Events for a Year

Some family-based youth ministries consider doing a once-a-month plan or "event" that is realistic and practical. Some youth events involve more hands-on experience, and others are selective and less intensive. Listed below is a compilation of a one-year plan.

January: State of the Union Address

This is a beginning-of-the-year informational meeting for parents that explains dates, costs, and events throughout the year. Parents always appreciate communication so they can plan accordingly.

February: Valentine's "Appreciation" Dinner with Youth Lock-in

The dinner is organized, cooked, served, and cleaned by the students for the parents! It is a night to thank and celebrate parents. When the meal is completed, the parents are free to enjoy a night without their teen because the youth ministry hosts a lock-in (parents' night off!), for which the students and adult volunteers will rent out a YMCA or gym and have food, games, and movies.

March: Parent Newsletter

Create a newsletter for all parents of middle and high school students. Include updates on events and mission trips and tips for parents on topics that interest them:

- How to listen to your teen so they want to talk

- What is happening in the youth culture

- How to talk so they will listen

- How to deal with bullies at school

- How to help my teen have a faith of their own

April: Seminar for Parents and Invite Parents to Youth Group

Bring in a local or national speaker to speak on the topic of helping parents grow in their skills of connecting with their teen. Homeword.com has an outstanding list of extremely practical seminars at reasonable prices. This is a three-hour seminar on a Saturday morning or Sunday late afternoon.

Make one day in April the Invite-a-Parent-to-Youth-Group Night. Many parents have never seen or heard what is going on at youth group, so spread the news and invite parents to come and watch. You might end up getting a few great volunteers in the process.

May: Parents and Teens Fun Night

Our town has a place called Frankie's Fun Park. It has go-carts and all kinds of games to play. Offer this kind of place for parents and teens to get crazy and silly (it's only two to three hours).

June: Off Nights for Youth Group

Because summers are busy for almost all Americans, cut back on the programming and scheduling. Perhaps cancel Sunday nights for a month or at least offer only one Sunday night program per month or offer activities on Sunday mornings instead (depending on how you organize things at your church). Off nights give parents (and teens) a chance to slow down a bit and take a break.

July: Mission Trip for Parents and Teens

Invite as many parents and teens as you can to be involved in a mission project together. It could be a local project that lasts one day or a regional project that lasts several days or an overseas project that lasts a week to ten days. It could be serving in a local homeless shelter or soup kitchen or taking a trip to Appalachia or to Costa Rica.

August: Mother-Daughter/Father-Son Night Out

There are probably a number of students whose parents are divorced or absent. Since this is like a mother-daughter and father-son event, kids with absentee dads or moms can "rent out" an adult to be a surrogate parent for the night. The night could involve games, tailgating, or dinner and a movie. We have taken guys and dads to monster truck night, played broomball, and headed to professional baseball or football games.

September: Half-Day Parent-Teen Retreat

This is not for the faint of heart and has the power to transform families. I have hosted or led hundreds of these retreats. I like to use low initiatives and ropes courses and perhaps a time of communion or foot washing (toward the end of the day) and prayer. Consider bringing someone as a facilitator.

October: Yard Work

Find people who are elderly and who might need help with yard work or home repairs, or enlist parents and their kids to help shut-ins on a Saturday or Sunday.

November: Have a Parent Advisory Committee

Ask some parents of students from each grade to meet once a semester for the purpose of asking one question: "How can youth ministry help families?" This is a time for parents to speak their minds and give helpful feedback.

December: Send E-Mail Devotions

Faith Five is a guided devotional for parents to have a brief (five-minute) discussion on the best and worst part of their day (done around dinner usually) and then one passage of Scripture. This gets the family talking about God's word related to their day. There are tons of devotionals available, and parents need help with learning how to discuss the Bible with their kids.[3]

9. Take On a New Paid Title and Position: Minister to the Whole Family

Youth workers educated from the 1970s to the 1980s generally were trained to work with teens only. We were called *youth director* or *youth pastor/minister*. However, we must now view youth ministry through a different lens. We should not only teach, counsel, and disciple teens but also seek to empower parents to lead their children. That means viewing parents as allies, not as adversaries. After spending over a decade in youth ministry with the working title *minister to youth*, I changed it to *minister to youth and families* and then later to *minister to youth and their parents*. Even though it sounds a bit awkward, the title communicated my purpose and mission—a calling to teens *and* their families. We must start early though. We shouldn't wait until parents knock down our doors when puberty hits their children.

The future of youth ministry is changing radically, and in order to keep up with the times, we must think strategically in our leadership. We can't afford to put our heads in the sand and pretend that problems will go away. Instead, let's be poised to make headway in helping teens and their families.

10. Parents Resourcing Parents

One of the best-kept secrets for parents of preteens and teenagers is one another. That's right. There are going to be times when a youth worker will not be able to provide insight or help. The most valuable resource to a struggling parent of an adolescent is another parent of an adolescent.

Sometimes parents are reluctant to share their problems with a youth worker, counselor, or lead pastor. I am telling you: parents helping parents is the most undervalued and least utilized tool in the body of Christ today. Encourage parents to talk with one another about what's happening in their families.

The Future Is Now

When I started in youth work in my twenties, I had no idea where we were headed concerning the future. Well, the future is now, and we must act. Our job as youth leaders is full, exciting, and complicated. No longer can we afford to work only with teenagers; we are becoming youth and family pastors and leaders.

I started the chapter by mentioning Sherry, who attended our youth retreat, only to be forbidden by her parents to attend church or youth group again. I am not saying that I could have changed the situation, but if I knew back then as a twenty-five-year-old what I know today thirty years later, I would have taken steps to meet the parents and try to establish a relationship. I would have at least taken a stab at connecting with the family.

God loves his church. He loves us personally and collectively. He cares about our students and their families and homes. We are to care as well. And may God equip us to be effective as we make disciples of Jesus of all people, including students and their families.

Transformation is God's plan for all of us, but this process will be limited with the traditional paradigm of student ministry as an island.

The future of youth ministry is the entire church ministering to the whole family.

Let's get this right.

Voices from the Trenches

"I was at a prayer meeting, and we were in small groups praying for people's needs. The guy next to me had this desperate look on his face and he said, 'I need God to give me some Bible verses to share with my kids at our bedtime devotions.' I was floored that this man cared so much to share God's word with his kids that he was asking the church (us) to help him love his family."

—Terrace, paid youth worker

Q's to Enhance

1. What can your church do to enhance families toward wholeness and balance?

2. Of the five families mentioned, which do you see the most? The least?

3. What's one step to have the entire church take to enhance families seriously?

Notes

1. Parts of this chapter appeared in the article "Scanning Beneath the Surface" by David Olshine in *Youthworker Journal* (May/June 1996): http://www.youthworker.com/youth-ministry-resources-ideas/youth-ministry/11646880.

2. Taken from "Living and Serving with Broken Hearts" by David Olshine in *Youthworker Journal* (November/December 2012): 12.

3. Ideas submitted by Columbia International undergraduate and graduate students: Howard Ki, Scott Miller, Caleb Hankin, Dora Adams, Allie Redmond, and Chris Leiby.

Chapter Twelve

WHO CARES FOR MY SOUL?

"Get busy living or get busy dying."
—Red, *in* The Shawshank Redemption

Bernie came to my office for counseling, feeling exhausted and burned out. "My pastor wants me to do youth ministry like he did thirty years ago. He wants me to totally pour out my soul to the student ministry. The problem is, I don't think I have anything left in the tank to pour out." Soul drought. Are you living or dying inside? Who cares for you, the soul giver?

What's the Problem?

My family travels frequently on long road trips, and when we drive by a deer sign, my son taps me on the shoulder and says, "There's a deer." I explain to him that it is only a picture and that the sign is cautioning us because deer have been spotted there. This driving scenario with Andrew happens all the time, and we've never seen a deer by these signs, that is, until yesterday. Andrew said *deer,* and he was right, with the exception that it was not alive but had become roadkill. There is a price to pay for not being attuned to the signs.

Warning signs are everywhere: *Keep out. No trespassing.* These are external boundaries, but how do we spot internal warnings for our *soul*? The "soul" is the deepest part of our being. Deuteronomy commands us to love and serve the Lord with "all our soul." Psalm 23 declares that the Lord our Shepherd "restores our soul." Jesus asks in Matthew 16:26,

"What good will it be for someone to gain the whole world, yet forfeit their soul?"

Signs instruct, teach, and warn. How do you know when *your* soul is in trouble? Are there signs that can alert us to imminent danger and keep us from going down the slippery slope?

Did Bernie Pay Attention to the Signs?

Bernie is not alone, trust me. Anyone who has any length of stay in youth ministry—whether that person is paid or is a volunteer servant-leader—has experienced fatigue and weariness of soul. The unique role of ministering to labor-intensive student ministry comes to this reality: we cannot give to students and families what we do not have.

When our souls are dry or empty, how do we give when there is nothing to offer? How do we refuel? Perhaps we had better start with another question, "What are some of the signs that *my soul* needs feeding?"

Here are some of my experiences plus insights from other youth workers when they have hit the wall:

- Little interest in prayer

- Loss of passion

- Bible reading like the *Wall Street Journal* (and the *Wall Street Journal* is actually more exciting!)

- Negativity

- Lack of sleep

- Restlessness of spirit

- Cynicism

- Constant discouragement

- Panic attacks or depression

- Comparison with others

- Never feeling successful enough

- Being relationally unmotivated

165

- Apathy

- Unresolved hurt

- Bitterness

- Stress

- Lack of exercise

- Ongoing failure or addiction in a particular area

- Lack of desire for ministry

- Disappointments and fears that won't go away

Recognize that some of these are "normal" and are part of being human, and having one or two of these symptoms does not determine an outbreak of a depleted soul. When a person, however, starts experiencing a number of these for several weeks, the chance of suffering exhaustion is heightened and soul care is warranted.

Problem #12 of American Youth Ministry:
The caretakers are not taking care of themselves.

In my mentoring and shepherding of youth leaders, especially those in their early to late twenties, I have noticed this group gets ramped up for lots of adventure and activity. Personally I think that is developmentally norma-tive and on target with the season of life they are in (I know I was driven this way). People in their twenties have lots of energy and adrenaline for the ride. Leaders in their twenties are primed and poised for movement and keeping the engine running, yet sometimes they are unaware the gas tank is empty (work with me on this analogy, please) and end up on the side of the road calling for help.

If a youth worker gets married, there is a newfound experience in learn-ing to manage more of life's tasks than ever before. And if parenting begins, the heat is on. We find ourselves doing more and more, and eventually we throw a gasket. I care not to mention how many people in "Christian minis-try" have had their family lives ruined because of missing the signs and then ignoring them. We are in the people business, and those in student ministry must take care of themselves.

Finding a Solution

Bernie may be a victim of a system, but he needs to find out how to be a victor. Here are ten recommendations for the "caretaker" to take care of himself or herself, in the same way that Bernie needs to take care of his soul.

Solution to Educate:
Establish boundaries, personal renewal, and soul care.

1. Taking Care of Your Whole Life Is Not Selfish

Life is about balancing and juggling. Housework, ministry to ourselves, exercise, family time, church, and vacations are all possible needs and values you have, and maturity is about learning how to systematize it all into manageable and sustainable rhythms. We need to begin with the first principle: it is not selfish to take care of your life. I mean, who came up with that? I have heard this from a number of people, and it's simply not true.

The book of Proverbs challenges us to be like the ants, that is, diligent in working hard and being disciplined: "Go to the ant, you sluggard; consider its ways and be wise! It has no commander, no overseer or ruler, yet it stores its provisions in summer and gathers its food at harvest" (Proverbs 6:6-8). The Scriptures teach that work is good and ordained by God. Adam and Eve had it made; their lives were a walk in the park. Work wasn't even work. But in Genesis 3, Adam and Eve sinned and work became…work: "Cursed is the ground because of you; through painful toil you will eat of it all the days of your life…. By the sweat of your brow you will eat your food until you return to the ground, since from it you were taken; for dust you are, and to dust you will return" (Genesis 3:17-19).

Notice the words associated with *work* after the fall of humanity: *painful toil* and *sweat of your brow*. Work before the fall evidently was fun and not tiring, and now it's laborious and painful.

Nonetheless, we are all called to work in a fallen world. And we serve a broken humanity as well. And we are broken. So to think only of myself on a 24/7 daily routine is selfish, but God has called each of us to take care of all that he has given us. We are stewards of our mind, body, and soul.

2. Understand Your Limits; Acknowledge Your Human Condition

The Johari window is an inventory that exposes how we see ourselves. The first view is self-view, which means this is what I see about me and what others do not see. The second view is what others see about me that I don't see about myself. The third view is what others see about me and I also see about me. The fourth view is what I don't see about myself and others don't see either, only God sees.

Youth leaders, to be healthy and vibrant physically, emotionally, and spiritually, must understand our limits. We must become self-aware of who we are and who we are not.

One of my favorite movies is *Rudy* (1993), which is about a struggling young man who wants to attend the University of Notre Dame and walk on as a football player. Rudy visits a Catholic priest and describes his passion for football and his concern that he might not get accepted into the prestigious school. The Father says, "Son, in thirty-five years of religious study, I have only come up with two hard, incontrovertible facts. There is a God and I am not him!"

A profound statement, isn't it? One, there is a God who orders the world, and two, it is not me. When I go to bed at night, God is not worried about or wondering what is next. God is not limited, but I am. Understand that in order to take care of your soul, you need to recognize where you are strong and where you are weak and be comfortable in your own skin. You don't have to be great at everything. Know your limits. Know your human condition.

3. Learn to Set Boundaries

Boundaries are markers that define the ebb and flow of life, and that is why we have lines on highways to delineate where we can drive and what is off-limits.

As I am a person in ministry, my highest relationship outside of Jesus is with my wife, Rhonda. One of the boundaries we have set as a married couple is to purposefully schedule a once-a-week twenty-four-hour day off from ministry tasks. It is a day to pray, play, and be with each other. Sometimes it involves a nap, exercise, walking in a park, lunch, or coffee. It is a clear boundary I set to communicate my love for my spouse. Typically I turn off my cell phone and usually keep all my technological gadgets off. There are other boundaries I set to care for my soul:

- I exercise four to five days a week.

- I go to bed around 11:00 p.m. each night (except during March Madness).

- I eat as healthy as possible.

- I never get in a car with a woman unless my wife is present.

- I never get in a car with a teenager unless several adults are present.

- I avoid any appearance that would raise unnecessary and unwarranted suspicion.

These boundaries might look restrictive and somewhat inconvenient, but the goal of a boundary is *protection*. Boundaries are guardrails; they protect us from going off the cliff.

Boundaries for Singles

Some of the greatest men and women in ministry are single, and creating boundaries as a single person is complicated. My friends tell me the most important decision they have made is *to have life outside of their ministry*. It is easy for a church or organization to take advantage of singles with this rationale: "They have more time than married people and nothing to do in their free time." Wrong answer! Singles have the same amount of time married folk do; how they use their time is different. Singles in ministry must learn boundaries just as much as those who are married.

Divorce- and Adultery-Proof Boundaries

For those who are married, don't settle for a marriage without excitement. Go on dates. Take every day of vacation you are allotted. Keep the fires of love, commitment, and passion burning in your marriage. Listen well to your spouse. Find out what communicates love to your spouse the most, whether it be gifts, affection, praise, or helping him or her in practical ways, and express this preferred love often.

Affairs happen frequently at work, so steer clear of hanging out with the opposite sex and casual flirting. One of my ministry friends just got rebuked by his ministry leader for texting a female worker in ministry. Words are so subtle and can give the wrong impression. Be careful and guard yourself. Be aware of the "appearance of evil." If you need to make a house visit, don't go alone. If you need to have a lunch meeting with a member of the opposite sex, take someone with you.

What is someone to think if you are hanging out with a gorgeous church worker? The Bible challenges us to flee temptation. If you find yourself in a tempting situation, do what the Bible says of Joseph when Potiphar's wife wanted to seduce him: he ran (Genesis 39:15). Here is some advice: if you find yourself staring in the face of a temptation that could potentially ruin your personal and professional life, *run!* When an enticement could sabotage your marriage, ministry, and ultimately your reputation and integrity, *run!* Flee!

If you have children, schedule special times with them. Mondays after school are my time with my son for eating at Wendy's, hitting the public library (he likes books), and going swimming in our indoor pool at the gym.

I have heard dying people say, "I wish I had more time with my family" or "I regret that I did not spend enough time with my spouse or kids." I have never heard anyone say, "I wish I had spent more time at the office." Never.

Voices from the Trenches

"First, both paid staff and volunteers need to serve in their areas of giftedness and build boundaries and margins into their lives. Even within youth ministry, youth pastors can 'play to their strengths,' which only increases fulfillment in ministry. This requires delegating to others those areas that are outside of our giftedness and inside other's giftedness. For example, if you don't like to shop for the fall retreat groceries, ask a parent who loves to organize and shop. Second, building boundaries into your personal and professional life will help you say yes and no at the right times and in the right ways. Margins, like those around the text on a page in a book, allow youth workers to save room for the unexpected and for times of reflection. If we cram our lives full, leaving little room for the unexpected and planned times of rest, we will burn out quickly. You certainly can't do it all on your own, and you have permission to think long-term for the sake of your spiritual health."

—Jeff, pastor of local outreach

4. There Are Times to Say, "Stop It"

The comedian Bob Newhart (playing Dr. Switzer) has a classic You-Tube video. A woman by the name of Catherine comes into his office for therapy. Dr. Switzer explains he charges only five dollars for the first five minutes and then following that charges nothing. While she explains in detail her "fear of being buried alive in a box," Dr. Switzer listens patiently and then has two words for her: "Stop it!" Catherine continues for the rest of the five minutes, complaining of bulimia, washing her hands too frequently, and her fear of driving. To all of the phobias, he yells, "Stop it!" The client becomes increasingly uncomfortable, frustrated, and discouraged. Finally she tells Dr. Switzer she doesn't like his style of counseling. He tells Catherine to pull out a piece of paper because he has ten words for her. She agrees, fumbling and digging into her purse for paper and pen. Dr. Switzer pauses, leans on the table, and then screams these words: "Stop it or I'll bury you alive in a box!"

I feel like saying, "Stop it!" to youth workers at lunch when every three minutes they're playing with their phone or looking at who called them. Stop it!

Take care of yourself and remember that busy-ness kills the soul. Where do you need to say to yourself, "Stop it"? Identify the areas, and then do it!

5. Access Your Priorities and Recalculate

I have a youth worker friend who used to call me three times a week with some sort of problem or issue to work through. I love this guy dearly, but finally I told him that he needed to respect my time a bit more and maybe only call once a week. I have had to text him with "On vacation" or "In a meeting. Will call back in a few days." What I was trying to communicate was my priorities and values.

What are your priorities? What stuff needs to be reduced, cut, or eliminated from your schedule?

I decided years ago that I would not let ministry rule me. I would make choices to protect my life and family. I am a professor at a Christian university, but I have a life outside of it. I have hobbies such as bicycling, reading, and traveling. My family and I love the mountains and the beach.

When I was thirty, I set a goal of visiting every state in the United States and thirty countries. I also set a goal of preaching and teaching in forty of those states, and I am about three short. Since I set a goal to visit thirty countries, i have racked up eighteen to date. These values are driven by my faith and energize my life.

My car and phone have global program services that let me know where I am travelling and when I am lost or off track. Sometimes we need a GPS to help us with goals in our life and ministry. What in your life is important to God? Here is some of my list:

- Time with Jesus daily or regularly

- Quality time with my spouse

- Hanging out with my children

- Dates with my wife like going to movies

- Exercising regularly

- Laughter and not taking myself so seriously

All of these deal ultimately with soul care. Do you have a value of reading or studying or praying or any of the above? It will take some assessing and prioritizing to get things done. Have you realized things cannot always be done in a day? We all have the same twenty-four hours a day and seven days a week. I have not met anyone who has eight days to get things completed. Check out your values and priorities. Recalculate if needed.

6. What Are You Eating?

Now I am meddling a bit, I know. We in youth ministry have a long history of pizza, soda pop, and chips and salsa. I mean, what teens want to show up to have broccoli, spinach, and grilled fish? Seriously, get control of what you are putting into your temple. We have seen from shows such as *The Biggest Loser* and from meeting up with trainers that we are not good to our bodies.

What we eat does affect our mood, our sleeping patterns, and our mental state. Too much sugar makes me sluggish, and certain kinds of foods can contribute to depression and ulcers. Watch what you eat. Be good to your body.

7. Learn to Balance Rest, Play, Work, and Prayer

Most people in the ministry (paid and nonpaid) cannot seem to relax without feeling guilty. I think the only way to be fully present to God and to people, but also to our families and our own needs, is to learn the complex balancing act called "living in tension."

We are not great at this, but we need to get better at balancing rest, play, work, and prayer.

Rest

My friend has a T-shirt that says, "Work hard, play hard, pray hard, rest hard." How does one rest hard? The first tangible area for youth workers is getting six to eight hours of sleep a night. Lack of sleep and insomnia contributes to poor performance in the work place and also can lead to migraines, anxiety, and despair.

Rest always involves creating times of pace and cadence to your daily existence. Slow down.

- Read a novel.

- Hit the tennis court.

173

- Drink coffee on your deck.

- Throw away your "to-do list" for a day.

- Have intentional downtime.

- Be bored and relish it.

Create a sustainable pace so that your body, soul, and spirit are not moving at a frenetic speed and one day you implode. My friend says, "Make sure you take every day of your vacation." Amen.

Play

Do you organize your schedule to occasionally have a getaway? If you are married, when was the last time you had a date night? How about an overnighter without the kids? Its okay to get away, okay? And don't take yourself so seriously all the time. Why do we need to educate ourselves when it comes to lightening up? Maybe it's because our world is so uptight. Lighten up.

When it comes to play, the blessing of having little children is that it keeps us doing fun and lighthearted events that we might normally avoid such as visiting water and amusement parks and just being silly. If you don't have children, find ways to do something crazy.

Work

Genesis communicates that God works. God created the universe and all of its beauty such as animals, stars, solar systems, and humans. God is Creator, and creating things takes work and time.

The Bible is clear that God *called us to work*. We see the first humans caring for the garden and naming the animals. Work is a good thing. God works. We work. Work is a biblical concept and happened before the fall of mankind. Having a high work ethic is vital to success, plus you cannot spend all your time playing and resting (I am guessing whatever vocation you have, you like and need the income).

A few years ago I met with a management expert for lunch. I was struggling with balancing my time in ministry, home life, speaking, and writing. Tom told me something I will never forget: "David, we are wired to work about fifty to sixty hours a week, and if you cannot accomplish most of your tasks for that week in that amount of time, you are probably not managing your time and resources wisely. After sixty hours, most people are probably just spinning their wheels."

One of the main Hebrew concepts of work was to start the day at sunrise and complete work at sundown. Following dinner, there would be a time of storytelling, eating, and laughter with the family then early to bed. Learn to say good-bye and allow God to run the universe. Your work is done; get some sleep and start refreshed the next morning.

Prayer

The most important relationship on earth for any youth worker is his or her relationship with Jesus. Take time regularly to nurture that relationship of love and intimacy with God because if you don't, your well will dry up and you won't have anything left to give students and families. "But when you pray, go into your room, close the door and pray to your Father, who is unseen. Then your Father, who sees what is done in secret, will reward you" (Matthew 6:6).

Get some alone time with God; find that secret place. It will feed your soul.

Voices from the Trenches

"It seems the reason youth leaders burn out is because they do not set the proper boundaries first. Many youth leaders make themselves 'accessible at any time,' which, on the surface, looks valiant. In all actuality, leaders need time alone to relax and spend time with God in order to refresh themselves so they can do their job to the best of their abilities. Others try to carry the burden of youth ministry all by themselves, which is too much for one person to handle. To battle this temptation, leaders must train and trust their volunteers to do some of the work with the kids for them. If they try to 'put the team on their back,' they will quickly learn that their backs are not strong enough."

—Wesley, high school student

---

8. Become a Proponent Concerning Sabbath

Exodus 20 is the introduction of the Ten Commandments to God's people. Keeping the Sabbath is in the same list as no lying, coveting, or committing adultery or murder. Look at the list:

Then God gave the people all these instructions:

"I am the Lord your God, who rescued you from the land of Egypt, the place of your slavery.

"You must not have any other god but me.

"You must not make for yourself an idol of any kind or an image of anything in the heavens or on the earth or in the sea. You must not bow down to them or worship them, for I, the LORD your God, am a jealous God who will not tolerate your affection for any other gods. I lay the sins of the parents upon their children; the entire family is affected—even children in the third and fourth generations of those who reject me. But I lavish unfailing love for a thousand generations on those who love me and obey my commands.

"You must not misuse the name of the LORD your God. The LORD will not let you go unpunished if you misuse his name.

"Remember to observe the Sabbath day by keeping it holy. You have six days each week for your ordinary work, but the seventh day is a Sabbath day of rest dedicated to the LORD your God. On that day no one in your household may do any work.... For in six days the LORD made the heavens, the earth, the sea, and everything in them; but on the seventh day he rested. That is why the LORD blessed the Sabbath day and set it apart as holy.

"Honor your father and mother. Then you will live a long, full life in the land the LORD your God is giving you.

"You must not murder.

"You must not commit adultery.

"You must not steal.

"You must not testify falsely against your neighbor.

"You must not covet your neighbor's house. You must not covet your neighbor's wife, male or female servant, ox or donkey, or anything else that belongs to your neighbor." (NLT)

Ministry can be toxic and addictive. Some leaders brag about how they don't take a day off. God gave these commandments because the Israelites had been slaves in Egypt for over four hundred years and never had a day off!

When reading Genesis 1–2, we discover that God created everything and then rested. Guess what, if God rests, then so do we. God did not make us human "doings" but human beings. We are called to "be" and not always "do." God calls us to be Sabbath-keeping people. The word *Sabbath* means "to cease or to stop."

God is active, but somehow after the creative process God took a break.

That does not mean God needs a nap, because he does not "sleep nor slumber." God was modeling for his created order a principle: work is good, and rest is needed.

The Pharisees were a religious group at the time of Jesus and were extremely dedicated to keeping the law of God, to the point of being rigid and even legalistic. One of the main contentions of the Pharisees with Jesus was any action or deed done on the Sabbath. They were over-the-top inflexible and strict about what was and wasn't done on "God's rest day" for humans.

Sabbath is not about rules; rather, it is about rest.

There are six days to work hard, but the seventh day is a Sabbath day of rest. God commands (not suggests) us to remember the Sabbath day by keeping it holy. *Holy* means "set apart, different." So if we work for six days, then day seven should look different and be set apart from the rest of the week because it is different. It is Sabbath.

I am not suggesting that youth workers become legalistic or Pharisaical about the Sabbath, but I am encouraging you to enthusiastically embrace the Sabbath. That means one day per week with no work. Be a proponent of the Sabbath, and advocate and promote it to all your colleagues, friends, and family. It will be good for your soul. When we truly embrace Sabbath, we are encountering God the Rest Giver.

Cease.

Stop.

Turn the cell phone off. Put the e-mails away. Go for a hike. Don't do ministry. Choose a day and try with all that is in your being to keep it. I have a friend who writes the words *DAY OFF* in his calendar every Tuesday. He makes sure he stays away from the office, and sometimes he spontaneously gets in his pickup truck and heads out of town for the day.

The Sabbath is both a day and an attitude. Jonathan works as a youth pastor on Sundays all day long, so Sunday is not his Sabbath. He and his wife have chosen Thursday as their Sabbath. Many Protestants and Catholics believe Sunday is the Lord's Day; whereas the Jewish community and Seventh-Day Adventists follow Saturday as the Sabbath. The Apostle Paul says in Romans 14:5: "One [person] considers one day more sacred than another; another...considers every day alike. Each one should be fully convinced in [their] own mind."

Each person must be fully convinced in his or her own mind, meaning this is a personal conviction and preference to the individual about the day he or she takes off and calls the "Sabbath." Just make sure you take one.

What should my attitude be concerning the Sabbath? Here are a few thoughts:

- Listen to God.

- Read the Bible for yourself and not for message preparation.

- Do something radically different on that day.

- Start a new hobby.

- Take a Sabbath from something: food, TV, computer, or complaining.

- Build a habit of being emotionally healthy.

- Sleep in!

- Be quiet as you walk in the woods.

- Establish a new rhythm for pacing yourself.

- Figure out why you say no and yes to certain things and discern if that's a good thing.

- Ask the question, "Are there things in my life I need to cut out in order to live my life simply and biblically?"

One of the best pieces of advice I received was given during graduation week from seminary. One of my professors stopped me and my roommate in the hall. He said, "I don't know you two very well, but I have been watching both of you for three years. I have an observation about you two." He continued, "David and Dan, you both have so much energy and passion and electricity in your DNA that I am fearful in five years you will be out of the ministry. So I want you both to make one promise to me. Please start out your ministry on the right foundation. Etch out on your calendar a day of no ministry, no church work, and no work, period. Set in stone a day off, a Sabbath. It will help your six days be productive, and you will be refreshed and renewed for the long haul. It may just save your life."

I committed to that principle years ago, and my professor was right—it has saved my life.

Sabbath is about rest, not rules.

9. Determine Your Mission and Live by It

Carving out a mission for your life is taking care of yourself. Over the years, I find myself continually defining and refining my mission. If your main assignment from God is your family and your job, stay within the parameters of that undertaking.

Too many youth leaders, volunteers, and parents go beyond the boundaries of what they can do well in a healthy manner, and that's when things get out of control and life falls apart, and people start going in all kinds of directions. Live by your mission from God.

10. Recognize Whether You Burn Out or Rust Out, Either Way, You Are Out

A friend used to say, "I am going all out for Jesus." Well, I think he did because he is out of the ministry due to fatigue and loss of passion he initially professed. Whether you are paid or are a volunteer or parent, you can give yourself to passion and time and energy, but know when to sign off, when to call it a night, when to move on and protect yourself from crumbling and collapsing.

If you are constantly burning the "midnight oil" without a break, you are not helpful to students or families, and especially not to your soul. Burn out or rust out—either way, you are toast.

Take care of yourself by establishing boundaries, personal renewal, and soul care.

Voices from the Trenches

"Water can only rise to its source. I was recently in Canada on the Welland Canal that takes ships from Lake Erie to Lake Ontario through the Niagara Peninsula. In twenty-six miles, the canal rises five hundred feet and is responsible for carrying over forty million tons of cargo each year! It does this through a series of locks that fill up with water to raise the enormous ships to the height of the next lock in the series. In the same way, youth leaders carry some heavy burdens in ministry. Burnout occurs when we don't have enough water to lift the burden. Avoiding burnout is directly related to our connection with Jesus the Living Water."

—Keith, paid youth worker

Q's to Educate

1. What kind of rhythm are you experiencing in your life?

2. What are some ways to incorporate rest, work, play, and leisure into your life?

3. What keeps you from setting boundaries for vacation and days off?

ABOUT THE AUTHOR

Dr. David Olshine is the Director of Youth Ministry, Family, and Culture at Columbia International University in Columbia, South Carolina, where he has been since 1993. A veteran youth worker, communicator, and professor, David is a much sought-after speaker around the country and has spoken to more than a million people. He has authored, contributed, and coauthored twenty books, including *Studies on the Go: Philippians, Colossians, 1 & 2 Thessalonians; Studies on the Go: Proverbs;* and *Tag-Team Youth Ministry.*

David is cofounder of Youth Ministry Coaches, an organization dedicated to coaching and consulting youth ministries. David is married "over his head" to Rhonda, and they have two awesome kids, Rachel and Andrew.

CPSIA information can be obtained at www.ICGtesting.com
Printed in the USA
LVOW13s0554110913

351676LV00004B/10/P